Cambridge Elements ☰

Elements in Bioethics and Neuroethics
edited by
Thomasine Kushner
California Pacific Medical Center, San Francisco

ART AND ARTIFICIAL INTELLIGENCE

Göran Hermerén
Lund University

CAMBRIDGE
UNIVERSITY PRESS

Shaftesbury Road, Cambridge CB2 8EA, United Kingdom

One Liberty Plaza, 20th Floor, New York, NY 10006, USA

477 Williamstown Road, Port Melbourne, VIC 3207, Australia

314–321, 3rd Floor, Plot 3, Splendor Forum, Jasola District Centre,
New Delhi – 110025, India

103 Penang Road, #05–06/07, Visioncrest Commercial, Singapore 238467

Cambridge University Press is part of Cambridge University Press & Assessment,
a department of the University of Cambridge.

We share the University's mission to contribute to society through the pursuit of
education, learning and research at the highest international levels of excellence.

www.cambridge.org
Information on this title: www.cambridge.org/9781009547789

DOI: 10.1017/9781009431798

First published 2024

A catalogue record for this publication is available from the British Library.

ISBN 978-1-009-54778-9 Hardback
ISBN 978-1-009-43178-1 Paperback
ISSN 2752-3934 (online)
ISSN 2752-3926 (print)

Art and Artificial Intelligence

Elements in Bioethics and Neuroethics

DOI: 10.1017/9781009431798
First published online: April 2024

Göran Hermerén
Lund University

Author for correspondence: Göran Hermerén, Goran.Hermeren@med.lu.se

Abstract: The overriding question discussed in this Element can be stated simply as: can computers create art? This Element presents an overview of the controversies raised by various answers to this question. A major difficulty is that the technology is developing rapidly, and there are still many uncertainties and knowledge gaps as to what is possible today and in the near future. But a number of controversial issues are identified and discussed. The position taken on controversial issues will depend on assumptions made about the technology, about the nature and location of consciousness, and about art and creativity. Therefore, a number of hypothetical answers are outlined, related to the assumptions made.

Keywords: art, artificial intelligence, creativity, values, consciousness

ISBNs: 9781009547789 (HB), 9781009431781 (PB), 9781009431798 (OC)
ISSNs: 2752-3934 (online), 2752-3926 (print)

Contents

1 Introduction   1

2 Who Is the Author?   12

3 Same or Different Learning Process?   21

4 Same or Different Creative Process?   28

5 Same or Different Kinds of Thinking?   33

6 Is It Art?   37

7 Concluding Remarks   54

   Notes   58

   References   62

1 Introduction

By way of introduction, some fairly recent controversies raised by the use of artificial intelligence (AI) to create images and texts are mentioned. This section is followed by a general description of AI programs for making images and a discussion of freedom and autonomy in AI programs and human life. The central problem discussed in this Element is stated, and its relevance for some other issues indicated.

1.1 Some Controversies

Computers have been used to make art for several decades. Recently, however, a number of events have been the subject of debate in the media. Artificial intelligence has entered the global art scene, but not without causing controversies and debates.

A game designer, Jason M. Allen, won first prize at the Colorado State Fair with his *Theatre D'Opéra Spatial*. This work was created using the AI tool Midjourney – which turns lines of text into realistic graphics. This sparked a controversy on social media, where critics called the award a threat to human artists everywhere. In an interview with *The New York Times*, Allen denied that he cheated, saying, 'I'm not going to apologize for it. . . . I won, and I didn't break any rules'.[1] In other interviews, he indicated that a way to avoid future controversy could be to separate AI-generated art from other kinds of art.

A fan sent rock artist Nick Cave a song written by the robot ChatGPT 'in Nick Cave style'. The ChatGPT's song included the chorus: 'I am the sinner, I am the saint / I am the darkness, I am the light / I am the hunter, I am the prey / I am the devil, I am the savior'. But the artist did not appreciate the lyrics, calling it 'bullshit' and 'a grotesque mockery of what it is to be human', according to an article in *The Guardian* (17 January 2023).

The singer wrote back to his fan, saying that 'dozens' of fans, 'most buzzing with a kind of algorithmic awe', had sent him songs produced by ChatGPT. 'Suffice to say, I do not feel the same enthusiasm around this technology', he wrote. 'I understand that ChatGPT is in its infancy but perhaps that is the emerging horror of AI – that it will forever be in its infancy, as it will always have further to go, and the direction is always forward, always faster.'

Christie's decision to sell a work of AI art, *Portrait of Edmond Belamy*, by the French art collective Obvious, in the autumn of 2018, has sparked debate over the status of the AI art movement.[2] Among many other things, the controversy raises the question of who the artist is and whether a new set of concepts is needed to determine authorship, rights and responsibilities.

In his comments on the Christie's auction of this work, Kieran Browne points out that the picture, printed on canvas and hung in a gilded frame, is aesthetically a very conservative work based on premodern aesthetics.[3] Nevertheless, it was sold for 432,500 US dollars. Christie's chose this work because of the limited human intervention in the creative process, claiming that the portrait was created by an algorithm and listed GAN (generative adversarial network) as the sole author of the work. Browne concludes that attributing authorship to the algorithm instead of to the hitherto rather unknown art collective Obvious turned out to be good business for Christie's.[4]

This text will focus on more basic and philosophical aspects than making judgements about the quality of an AI-generated rock song, discussing whether AI will put artists out of work and/or whether AI-generated pictures should be a category of their own at exhibitions, auctions and competitions. In order not to beg any questions as to whether the pictures or objects generated by AI software are art or not (this is an issue that will be discussed later separately), I will avoid expressions like 'AI-generated art' and instead – when the focus is on the visual arts – write 'AI-generated pictures' or 'AI-generated images'.

1.2 AI Programs for Making Pictures

A major difficulty is that the technology is developing so rapidly; it is difficult, if not impossible, to keep abreast of the changes. However, some basic information about the possibilities may be useful to readers interested in the topic but not at all familiar with the possibilities of using AI to generate pictures. To simplify, I will mainly focus on the visual arts; other forms of art like music and literature may raise somewhat different issues.

Moreover, even though the technology is in rapid flux, the philosophical questions about the nature, definitions and criteria of art are as puzzling as ever, particularly as they are now challenged not only by post-modern contemporary art forms but also by the use of AI in producing pictures. The issues concern, among other topics, the role of art in our lives and the relation between the arts and 'the human condition'.

In general terms, AI is used to analyse large amounts of information and to find patterns in this information. Pictures are fed into a computer program. Each picture is provided with a label, for instance 'face', 'dog' or 'landscape'. On the basis of the patterns found, the program can recognize and classify new pictures as pictures of dogs, even if the program has not been fed that particular picture of a dog before.

The development of new programs is fast. Examples include Nightcafé, Midjourney, Stable Diffusion, Disco Diffusion, Dall-E2, DreamStudio,

DreamStation and DeepDream (Google). Artificial intelligence research and development is taking place in a rapidly growing number of places, including Helsinki, Rutgers/New Brunswick, Seattle, San Francisco, Tübingen and Zurich.

Within the broad category of digitally manipulated pictures, there are several developments. Sometimes a distinction is made between weak and strong AI. Weak AI will carry out tasks according to instructions provided by the user. New pictures can be created using others as a point of departure, but precise instructions ('prompts') are needed. A program like Midjourney begins by creating four different versions of each picture fed into the program. The user can then choose one of these for further processing. Jeff Hayward has used DALL-E to recreate paintings by other famous artists, for instance, the *Mona Lisa* in the style of Matisse.

Another AI program, used by Karl Sims, functions as follows.[5] The program selects (or is fed) a picture, which it processes. The algorithm creates nineteen new pictures using the first picture as a point of departure. Then the user can combine the first picture with any of the nineteen pictures created by the program, or choose one of the nineteen new pictures as a starting point, and let the program process this picture and generate nineteen new ones. The process can be repeated by the users as many times as they like. The more times the process is repeated, the more difficult it will be to recognize the picture used as a starting point.

Within weak AI, it is possible to distinguish between different degrees depending on the kind and number of activities performed by the user concerning the choice of pictures, the precision and amount of instructions, the number of iterations made before the user is satisfied with the outcome, more or less extensive uses of Photoshop and so forth.

'Strong AI' differs from weak AI in that a strong AI program analyses large amounts of pictures created by others, can perform a variety of functions, and is able to generate new algorithms (that is, a new set of rules to be followed in calculations or other activities) and/or write its own programs. Obviously, this raises many questions for further consideration. There are also differences in the literature about the precise relations between strong and weak AI at present.

For the time being, I will leave open the question of whether the difference between weak and strong AI is one of degree or kind, as well as speculations on future developments. Incidentally, the distinction between 'degree' and 'kind' is not crystal-clear and may be relevant for some of the controversies discussed in Section 6. Various labels may be used, and related distinctions are described in somewhat different ways. Yet it seems that there is more or less agreement in the literature on the differences between several uses of AI to generate pictures. Marian Mazzone and Ahmed Elgammal write as follows: 'In contrast to traditional algorithmic art, in which the artist had to write detailed code that already specified the rules for the desired aesthetics, in this new wave, the algorithms are set up by artists to 'learn' the aesthetics by looking at many images using machine learning technology'.[6]

How is it done? What is the procedure used? The user has three roles or tasks: pre-curation, tweaking the algorithm and post-curation:

> The artist chooses a collection of images to feed the algorithm (pre-curation), for example, traditional art portraits. These images are then fed into a generative AI algorithm that tries to imitate these inputs. The most widely used tool for this is generative adversarial networks. . . . In the final step, the artist sifts through many output images to curate a final collection (post-curation).

In this phase, it seems clear that the user is the artist and the author of the images generated:

> In this kind of procedure, AI is used as a tool in the creation of art. The creative process is primarily done by the artist in the pre- and post-curatorial actions, as well as in tweaking the algorithm. There have been many great art works that have been created using this pipeline. The generative algorithm always produces images that surprise the viewer and even the artist who presides over the process.[7]

But Mazzone and Elgammal also describe a new third phase in development, where they suggest that their program AICAN is an '(almost) autonomous artist':

> At Rutgers' Art & AI Lab, we created AICAN, an almost autonomous artist. Our goal was to study the artistic creative process and how art evolves from a perceptual and cognitive point of view. . . . The machine is trained between two opposing forces – one that urges the machine to follow the aesthetics of the art it is shown (minimizing deviation from art distribution), while the other force penalizes the machine if it emulates an already established style (maximizing style ambiguity). These opposing forces ensure that the art generated will be novel but at the same time will not depart too much from acceptable aesthetic standards.[8]

In the last sentence of this quotation, they use 'art' rather than 'picture', thereby taking a position on the classification of the outcome. They underline the difference between the earlier generative phase and the new creative phase:

> Unlike the generative art discussed earlier, this process is inherently creative. There is no curation on the dataset; instead we fed the algorithm 80 K images representing 5 centuries of Western art history, simulating the process of how

an artist digests art history, with no special selection of genres or styles. The creative process using CAN is seeking innovation. The outputs surprise us all the time with the range of art AICAN generates.[9]

But is art made by 'Deep Learning' techniques, such as GANs, different from art made by other generative algorithms? While some researchers, such as Mazzone and Elgammal, underline the differences, others emphasize similarities. For instance, Jon McCormack et al. answer the question about differences as follows:

> There are no significant new aspects introduced in the process or artefact of many GAN produced artworks compared to other established machine learning systems for art generation. Currently, there is a difference in the way GANs are presented by media, auction houses and system designers: as artificially intelligent systems that is likely affecting the perception of GAN art. As this difference is grounded more in terminology and marketing than intrinsic properties of the technique, history suggests it is not likely to sustain.[10]

Clearly, there are some differences in the descriptions of AI technologies used to generate pictures. Aaron Hertzmann describes the spectacular development of computational artistic image synthesis from Photorealistic Rendering, via Neural Style Transfer, the invention of DayDreams, up to Generative Adversarial Networks and Creative Adversarial Networks and concludes: '*In each of these cases, the artworks are produced by a human-defined procedure, and the human is the author of the imagery.*'[11]

Hertzmann summarizes his position as follows: 'I do not believe that any software system in our current understanding could be called an artist. Art is a social activity.'[12] However, I will not take a position on this issue here, but in a later section (Section 6).

1.3 Freedom and Autonomy in AI Programs – and in Human Life

Some of the early AI programs only did what the instructions of the user/programmer told them to do, for instance 'a still life in impressionist style'. It can then be argued that in this case, there is a strong causal relation between the instructions and the outcome, defined in terms of some combination of the concepts necessary and/or sufficient conditions.

However, there are more advanced computer programs where the relationship between the instructions and the outcome is more indirect; the outcome can be difficult or impossible to predict and may even surprise the programmer. Some – including myself – may be prepared to assume that there is a weak and indirect causal relation between the outcome and the user's instructions. The challenge is then to identify and define this indirect causal relation.

In the general description in Section 1.2 of the recent development of AI programs for generating pictures, there are a few key statements that require extra attention because hypothetical answers to the philosophical, ethical and legal problems stated in the introduction can be based on them. Artificial intelligence programs can (appear to) make surprising decisions and produce outcomes not explicitly designed into the software by the programmer. This process needs to be clarified. How is this apparent freedom of action to be understood? Does it mean that AI programs can make decisions of their own?

The answer will have implications for military issues as well. According to reports in the media in June 2023, drones were first programmed to achieve certain goals (to destroy target X). Then they were provided with instructions not to destroy that target. Tests in the United States indicated that drones could act in counter to these new instructions. Do the drones make decisions of their own not to obey instructions that are incompatible with previously given instructions? Or are they programmed to do so?

How Free Are You? This is the title of a book by Ted Honderich in which he comments on several much-discussed factors limiting our freedom of choice and action, such as childhood experiences and genetic profile. Can we ask the same question about computer programs? What would it require for this question to be meaningful? Certainly, computers do not have childhood experiences and DNA.

As Margaret Boden points out, 'The notion of autonomy or self-direction is implicit in talk of someone's "originating" an idea. Indeed, creativity is often thought of as a species of freedom.'[13]

But 'freedom' and 'autonomy' are ambiguous words. Boden distinguishes between two different kinds of autonomy in non-technological contexts and their parallels in image-generating AI programs/computational art: (1) physical autonomy as exhibited in homeostatic biological systems, and (2) mental/intentional autonomy as exemplified by human free will:

> For our purposes, however, the most important difference is that between autonomy *as ascribed to non-human systems* and autonomy *as ascribed to adult human beings* (though not to babies or infants). The latter form has a special name of its own: freedom.
>
> Human freedom is a special case of self-organization that's commonly regarded as the epitome of autonomy.[14]

Here, freedom (1) is underpinned by self-organization, which Boden views as synonymous with a specific kind of autonomy where 'the system's independence is especially strong: it is not merely self-controlled, but also self-generated'[15] – with the 'self' in self-organization referring to the impersonal components of the system, not the intentional, mental self. But freedom (2) is inherently tied to human freedom: something lacking in the autonomy of AI picture-generating systems.

Analysis of human freedom presupposes a context of reasoning, motivation, plans and decisions. The reasoning includes an analysis of possible obstacles and difficulties on the road towards the goal and possible ways of eliminating, reducing and circumventing them. Freedom of this kind is relevant when the focus is on the possibility of humans to choose and carry out different projects.

Human freedom, according to Boden and others, must be distinguished from freedom in the self-organizing sense. Indeed, there are advanced computer programs that can change themselves in response to external stimuli. They can learn and adapt. Consequently, they can do things that will surprise the programmer – that is, do things that the programmer never anticipated or designed into the software, and may even involve the development of values/preferences very different from those of the programmer.

According to Boden, 'The program may contain rules for *changing itself*. For example, it may be able to learn – perhaps on the basis of unpredictable input from the environment, or perhaps due to its self-monitoring of internal "experimentation" of various kinds. Or, more to the point for our purposes here, it may contain genetic algorithms.'[16]

But what are the limits of this freedom, and who sets them? If this is done by the programmer or the software engineer, it can be argued that the freedom, at least indirectly, is determined by the instructions of the programmer. Thus, a case can be made for saying that the author of the images generated is the programmer. Boden concludes, 'So we must allow that, *in that strictly limited sense*, no programmed system can be truly autonomous.'[17]

Saying that a computer-based information-processing system is autonomous does not make it autonomous in all senses of that ambiguous word. Boden makes an important comment on the way 'autonomy' is sometimes used:

> ... some AI scientists – and some computer artists too – actually make a point of describing their systems as "autonomous." In saying this, they are highlighting certain interesting features of the ways in which their machines function ... asserting some degree of independence on the machine's part. But they are not all focusing on the same features, so they are using the term "autonomous" in three very different senses to denote distinct types of processing – only one of which is at all analogous to human freedom.[18]

In a review of Boden's *Creativity and Art*, Berys Gaut makes the following comment: 'For instance, if, as she notes, our appreciation of art depends on the attribution of autonomy to the artist, then her distinction between non-human autonomy and autonomy as freedom shows that appeal to the autonomy of computer art may be equivocal, since it is freedom that is relevant to the issue of art, not mere self-organization'.[19]

To sum up so far:

We should distinguish between at least two senses of autonomy: non-human autonomy (more broadly, self-organization) and autonomy as freedom (the intentional-mental sense of freedom, which requires reasoning, planning and motivation).

Autonomy in the self-organizing sense:

Explains in what sense and how programs can adapt and learn, creating surprising output that is also surprising to the programmer.

Autonomy in the human freedom sense:

Explains how humans could be free in the sense that they could have chosen differently, if they had chosen to make the choice, in a context of plans, motivations and reasoning about alternatives, consequences and probabilities.

On the basis of this distinction, the following assumptions may be made:

(A) Autonomy in the self-organizing sense occurs in some advanced AI programs, which can learn and adapt, change themselves and react to external stimuli in ways not foreseen by the programmer, as described earlier in this section. But it can be argued that this kind of autonomy is neither necessary nor sufficient for creating art.

(B) Autonomy in the human freedom sense is required or can occur when human artists create works of art. It can be argued that this kind of autonomy is necessary but not sufficient for the creation of art, or at least part of a necessary condition for creating art.

Some may be inclined to object to these assumptions, for instance, on the basis of definitions and theories of art. If this disagreement cannot be settled, the question of whether computers can create art must be left open for the time being.

Jon McCormack et al. conclude their discussion of autonomy as follows:

> Thus any claims we can make about the autonomy of a GAN-based software system's autonomy are limited. Certainly, many different generative systems with equal or greater autonomy exist (in the non-intentional sense). While a claim such as 'an AI created this artwork' might be literally true, there is little more autonomy or agency that can be attributed to such an act than would be to a situation where 'a word processor created a letter', for example.[20]

The concept 'decisions of its own' requires further discussion. A related key statement surfaces in Mazzone and Elgammal's description of the functions of their AICAN: 'For each image it generates, the machine chooses the style, the subject, the forms, and composition, including the textures and colors.'[21] The keyword here is 'chooses'. We may have a rough idea of what it means when we talk about human choices. But what does it mean when this word is applied to computers or their software? Does it mean that there are no obstacles and that the programs would have chosen the style, the subject and so forth, if it had chosen to make the choice?

The sentence from Mazzone and Elgammal, quoted in the previous paragraph, is qualified by a preceding remark by the authors: 'Here, we posit that the person(s) setting up the process designs a conceptual and algorithmic framework, but the algorithm is fully at the creative helm when it comes to the elements and the principles of the art it creates'.[22]

The first part of this sentence raises the question of what limitations, if any, the conceptual and algorithmic framework imposes on the choices made by the software.

Does a picture-generating AI program process the information it is fed in such a way that it makes sense to argue that the program is experiencing something, understands what it is doing, and to some extent is conscious of itself, its emotions and its values? Processing information does not presuppose experiences and consciousness of the kind indicated by this question. Of course, some researchers and artists may be inclined to assume that this – or the contrary – is the case, but then these assumptions should be made explicit, if possible, argued for, and not be presented as proven facts.

What goes on in the AI program? Not even the person designing the program will always be able to predict the outcome. Therefore, we need to distinguish between predictability and autonomy. The fact that a picture-generating AI program, after a number of iterations, may generate pictures surprising even to the programmer should not be unexpected. As indicated earlier in this section, this does not mean that the system is autonomous in a sense we may attribute to humans when they make autonomous artistic and aesthetic choices. The fact that the outcome can surprise the programmer and the user does not exclude that there is an indirect and weak causal connection between the instructions of the user and the outcome.

The lack of transparency makes it difficult to tell whether any particular precise interpretation of statements such as 'There are AI programs that make their own decisions' is justified, and whether there is strong evidence for the statement interpreted in that way. This is a reason for making explicit the assumptions made about the possibilities of the technology and providing hypothetical answers to the problem related to these assumptions.

1.4 The Central Problem and Its Relevance for Some Other Issues

The main issue to be addressed in this text can be stated simply as: 'Can computers create art?' This can be more specifically rephrased as: 'Can computer-based information-processing systems create art?'

Who is the author of images generated by an AI program? Is it the programmer, the user, the program, the algorithm or the manufacturer? The answers to these questions will have implications for a number of philosophical, ethical and legal issues, including the following:

Philosophical issues: Can any of the many theories about consciousness developed and discussed during the history of philosophy be applied to picture-generating AI programs so that it is plausible to conclude that some of these programs can have consciousness, including experiences, interests and intentions?

Ethical issues: Who is to be blamed or praised if an AI-generated picture turns out to be obscene, offensive or horrible – or if it is spectacular and breaks new ground? Is it the software, the programmer, the user, the owner, the manufacturer or any combination of these? And if so, in what proportion?

Economic issues: Who is entitled to receive the income – or at least get a share, and if so how much – from sales or exhibitions of AI-generated pictures? The programmer, the user, the owner, the manufacturer, or any combination of these, and if so, in what proportion?

Legal issues: Are AI art generators copyright infringers? Who owns the Intellectual Property Rights (IPR) to the work and can sue those who plagiarize AI-generated pictures? The programmer, the user, the owner, the manufacturer or any combination of these? And if so, in what proportion? Concerning IPR, it is essential to separate the possible rights of the AI user from the IPR of those artists whose pictures have been fed into AI programs and used to 'train' the program.

Some comments. Artificial intelligence programs for generating pictures are 'trained' on pictures, which may already be protected by copyright or other forms of IPR. This suggests a choice. Should artists be required to *opt in*, that is, actively consent to this use of their works? That is, it is assumed that they do not consent if they have not done so explicitly. Alternatively, should they be required to *opt out*? That is, it is assumed that they consent unless they make clear that they do not consent. Recently, moves from opt in towards opt out have been made in European Union (EU) legislation, but the implications need to be followed up. What do those who violate these rights have to pay if prosecuted and convicted? What is fair and reasonable, and on what grounds?

Both responsibility for something that happened or was done in the past (backward-looking responsibility) and for what is to be done in the future (forward-looking responsibility) require knowledge of causal connections ('whose actions caused or are likely to cause X?') as well as what agents and stakeholders believed – or had good reason to believe – about the outcome of their actions. Clearly, there are uncertainties and knowledge gaps here. Knowing how advanced AI programs are constructed is essential, but a difficulty is that probably only the programmer knows this well. Nevertheless, sometimes even the programmer is surprised by the outcome, as already mentioned. This makes it difficult to handle problems of responsibility in a clear and fair manner.

In this discussion, we may sometimes consider the output, for instance, the images generated, and sometimes the process of creation. Both need to be examined. Is the question of responsibility different if we compare AI programs and their output to animals, for instance, primates taking photos or making paintings? Probably not. If we focus first on legal responsibility, the legal systems I am familiar with would not regard primates and AI programs as responsible for what they do. As to judgements about moral responsibility, it may be argued that they require the ability to reason logically, to anticipate the consequences of actions, and perhaps also the ability to feel regret.

Whether we focus on legal or moral responsibility, it is important to avoid situations where nobody is responsible for what an AI program has generated. Different kinds of joint responsibility may have to be explored, depending on what exactly the various agents and stakeholders have contributed to the outcome: the user, the programmer, the programs used, the manufacturer, and/ or the regulatory authorities. Perhaps this could be done in terms of actions and omissions being necessary and jointly sufficient for the outcome, plus clauses about the extent to which the outcome could be foreseen and avoided by those involved.

Another issue that needs further discussion and analysis is this: who can be holders of IPR? So far, traditionally only humans, not apes making paintings, not machines, but only those who have invented, manufactured or used machines. Does this apply to computers or computer programs, or are changes in the legal system required? If so, on what grounds? Or do we need to change our assumptions about computers and computer programs and say they are so similar to humans that they can create original works of art? If this is so, computer programs should also be considered as holders of rights. Then the images they have generated could enjoy the protection of IPR if the usual patentability requirements are met.

2 Who Is the Author?

2.1 Introduction

In this section, I discuss various possible answers to the question as to who the author is of a work generated by an AI program. The answer is obviously relevant to some of the problems mentioned at the end of the previous section. Authorship disputes are common in research, and I begin by exploring analogies to the criteria of authorship in scientific publications. Then I identify the main candidates in this context and discuss the extent to which they may qualify as authors or contributors. The idea that the computer program itself can be the author is controversial, and some assumptions used to support this position are discussed at the end of this section.

2.2 The Issue

David Hockney has used a computer (his iPad) as a tool to produce drawings. There can be no discussion about who the author of the images is, having seen the instructive documentary of the process: www.hockney.com/index.php/works/digital/ipad. But an obvious and important controversy concerns who the author is when, for instance, advanced AI programs have been used to generate pictures, since many people are involved or have contributed to the outcome.

Thus, the first controversy I will comment on can be stated simply as:

(1) Who is the author of a work created by an AI program?

The obvious candidates in this context – when AI programs are used to generate pictures – include the user, the programmer/the software engineer, the trainer and the program or algorithm itself.

The answer to (1) has consequences for many of the ethical, economic and legal problems mentioned at the end of Section 1.

2.2.1 Determining Authorship

What criteria could be used to settle authorship disputes? A reasonable starting point for the discussion of this issue could be comparisons with criteria of authorship in other areas, such as scientific research. The Vancouver recommendations are widely used and include definitions of the roles of authors and contributors.

According to the Vancouver recommendations, authorship shall be based exclusively on the following four criteria:

- substantial contributions to the conception or design of the work, or the acquisition, analysis or interpretation of data for the work
- drafting the work or revising it critically for important intellectual content

- final approval of the version to be published
- agreement to be accountable for all aspects of the work in ensuring that questions related to the accuracy or integrity of any part of the work are appropriately investigated and resolved.

Contributors who have contributed to a scientific publication but whose contributions do not justify authorship are to be described clearly in a contributorship statement. As suggested by some medical journals, such contributions could be 'served as scientific advisors', 'critically reviewed the study proposal', 'collected data' or 'provided and cared for study patients'.

But this is only a starting point, bearing in mind that there are significant differences in publication practices between disciplines and no universally accepted standards for assigning authorship. Nevertheless, it may be worthwhile to consider possible applications of and analogies to these criteria when computer programs are used to generate pictures.

As already mentioned, the obvious candidates in this context include the user, the programmer/the software engineer, the trainer and the program or algorithm itself. In what follows are some introductory comments on these candidates.

The user. It may be suggested that there are analogies to some of the clauses of the Vancouver recommendations when AI programs are used to generate pictures. The user of the program – especially if the programs are of the sort that can be instructed to make, say, a still life in Renaissance style – can qualify as the author of the outcome. This is particularly the case if the user selects among the pictures obtained and uses some of them as starting points for generation of new pictures in a process that can be repeated many times (as the earlier description of the working methods of Karl Sims suggests). Then it can be suggested that the user contributes substantially to the outcome of the process. The user can certainly also make the final adjustments and approve of the final version to be published.

The programmer. A software engineer or programmer could contribute substantially to the development or the design of the program used to generate pictures. But it may not always be easy to know where to draw the line in cases where the software used builds on software previously developed by others. The person(s) who trained and modified parameters can be considered to be contributors as well. This is also suggested by McCormack et al.[23]

The trainer. Likewise, those who train the programs by feeding pictures might also be regarded as contributing authors, or perhaps contributing non-authors. But what about artists whose works feature prominently in the training data? Can they also be considered as authors or contributors? Similar problems also occur in other situations, for instance concerning texts used as sources.

A general answer seems difficult to justify. Whether these other artists should be considered to be authors or contributors might, in the final analysis, depend on how prominently their works figure in the images created and how recognizable their contributions are.

The AI program. Can a computer program or an algorithm make 'a final approval of the version or picture to be published'? Or can it 'agree to be accountable for all aspects of the work in ensuring that questions related to the accuracy or integrity of any part of the work are appropriately investigated and resolved'? It seems that these questions will have to be answered negatively, unless we are prepared to attribute various mental capabilities to algorithms or programs. Some researchers seem prepared to do that, while others do not. Thus, there are arguments on both sides.

But personally, I have not been convinced by the arguments used to support these attributions. It is true, as stressed by Boden and others, that AI programs can be programmed to change themselves, to interact with external stimuli and to change themselves in surprising ways. This has already been discussed in the previous section. But this does not imply that we have to attribute mental capabilities like thinking, comparing, concluding, and making decisions to computer programs.

An alternative to attribute consciousness and other mental capabilities to AI programs could be to think in terms of causal requirements and use the conceptual framework discussed by John Mackie: necessary conditions, sufficient condition and in particular what Mackie refers to as inus-conditions: *insufficient* but *non-redundant* part of an *unnecessary* but *sufficient* condition.[24] Each single factor in a complex formula of the sort described by Mackie can be related to the outcome in an important way, as an inus-condition.

It could be tempting to apply this conceptual framework to the analysis of the indirect and weak causal connections that could occur also in advanced AI programs between the instructions of the user or programmer and the surprising outcome of the process. But whatever conceptual framework is used to describe what those have done who, in various ways, contributed to generating pictures via computers, it is important to be transparent about who has contributed what. These descriptions can then be the basis or starting point for drawing the lines between authors, contributing authors and non-author contributors. This discussion has only started and will have to continue as the technology is rapidly changing.

Some problems. A comparatively simple situation would be the one when the software engineer, the developer of the program, the user and the person training the program by feeding it pictures, as well as the person who has created the pictures fed to the computer, are one and the same. But that is rarely, if ever, the case. Usually, many people are involved, directly or indirectly, in the creation of what is labelled as AI art. Then the contributions of each person have to be specified as adequately as possible.

One of the problems discussed in this context is that the AI programs used to generate the outcome, such as pictures, can (a) have several authors and (b) be based on other earlier programs that also may have several authors. It may therefore be difficult to draw a clear line between contributing authors, non-author contributors, and those who should not be regarded as contributors.

Part of the controversy raised by the Christie's auction mentioned in the introduction centred on the uncredited use by the art collective Obvious of the software written by Robbie Barrat. If his software was a necessary condition for the creation, or part of a sufficient condition, Barrat could be considered a contributing author of the work. But the picture is complicated. Barrat's software was itself based on software made by others and ultimately traceable to the original GAN by Ian Goodfellow. Thus, many other artists and software engineers had contributed to the work by Obvious without getting credit or revenue, as Browne mentions in his comments on the auction.[25]

Accordingly, it is very clear in my view that there is no general answer to the main question discussed in this section, (1) 'Who is the author of a work created by an AI program?' that is valid for all cases. A well-considered answer has to be related to what AI software is used and what the various agents, the software engineer, the user and others, have contributed in each particular case. This needs to be specified.

The answer to (1) will therefore differ due to several factors. In other words, when there are several different contributors, the roles and responsibilities of each of them, as well as the credit due to them, need to be clarified. Accurate and inclusive attribution is essential from an ethical point of view. In research ethics, there has been a debate about such issues, with some controversies as a starting point.

The merit value of being author. Determining authorship is important for several reasons. It has a merit value for academics and artists. Authorship issues need to be put in a legal and ethical context. Schematically, if certain conditions are met, X is entitled to be regarded as the author of Y. Moreover, if X is entitled to be regarded as the author of Y, then X has certain roles, rights and responsibilities – and others (reviewers, editors, colleagues) have responsibilities and duties towards X.

Thus, controversies over authorship raise not only legal and economic problems of the sort mentioned at the end of Section 1 but also a number of ethical issues, including but not limited to assignments of rights and responsibilities. A basic question then concerns the value of being an author. Raising this question places the debate in a historic, cultural and legal context, as McCormack et al. also point out.[26]

Recommendations concerning best practice have to be stated with this in mind. In publication ethics, there are the already mentioned Vancouver recommendations. Something similar to these recommendations – regularly updated to be in touch with societal changes and new developments in research and technology – would be useful also in the area of AI-generated images. When AI is used for this purpose, similar issues of recognition, merit value, conflicts of interest and the right to part of the revenue from sales and shows are at stake.

A complication. In many cases, when AI programs have been used to generate images, AI is clearly a tool, as already suggested. The user of the program is the author of the output and the one deserving credit or criticism. But this may not be so clear when more advanced AI software is used. As mentioned earlier, there are advanced computer programs that can change themselves in response to external stimuli. These programs have the potential to learn and adapt; they have autonomy in what Boden called 'the self-organizing sense'.[27] Hence, they can surprise the programmers by outcomes that the programmer never anticipated. Here, the situation becomes more complex.

Can an algorithm be considered to be the author? Advanced AI programs can surprise the programmers and have the potential to act in ways that were not part of the initial programming, as already mentioned. Should the notion of authorship be extended to the algorithms in these situations so that they are recognized at least as partial or contributing authors? Some researchers, including Philip Galanter,[28] seem to be willing to defend this approach, while others, such as Anthony O'Hear, are not.[29]

2.3 Contested Assumptions

Regarding AI computer programs as authors would seem to require that we attribute to the programs some degree of awareness of their intentions, emotions and values as well as a certain autonomy in the human freedom sense. To many, this seems counterintuitive and hard to digest. However, there are arguments on both sides. For example, McCormack et al. state, 'There is nothing in principle that dismisses the possibility of artificial creative systems possessing this intentional autonomy ... '.[30]

Crediting AI tools or algorithms with authorship would imply that we should treat them as persons. This is clearly acknowledged by Galanter: 'Moving from the normative realm of aesthetics to that of ethics, this article considers when humans will be morally obliged to recognise AIs as ethical agents worthy of rights and due consideration.'[31] Those who argue in favour of the claim that an AI tool should be considered to be an author, like Galanter, point out that we cannot exclude that AI programs could be sentient and thus could have interests that we are morally obliged to take into account: 'But there is nothing that presently proves machine sentience is impossible. Machine consciousness remains an open question. As such, a sense of due diligence should oblige us to extend patiency to apparently aware machines as our own moral obligation'.[32]

However, this argument seems at present to me to be too weak for attributing authorship to computers or rather computer programs. The conceptual change Galanter proposes is not insignificant, and it requires more solid evidence. Moreover, Galanter makes the point that: 'Unlike most generative systems, an AI capable of autonomous learning, exploration, and realization of works has no dependency on its programmer for its creative direction, techniques, content, or aesthetics. These are all aspects of what we expect from human authors, not traditional generative art systems.'[33] In his statement, it seems that Galanter is taking for granted what should be proved or supported by independent evidence.

2.4 Is Consciousness Required?

Do we have to assume that in order to be an author of a text, a picture or a computer program, it is necessary to have experiences and be able to express emotions – and in that sense be sentient and conscious of something, at least to some minimal degree? In that case, we need to consider some assumptions about the notion, origin and location of consciousness, including also that consciousness can have different objects (conscious of this X but not of that Y) and be graded.

A problem discussed in some detail by Boden and others[34] is that there are many mutually incompatible theories and definitions of consciousness. For these reasons, I will avoid the general and abstract noun 'consciousness' and in each case specify the object of consciousness, allegedly what the algorithm or the program might be aware of. What I want to suggest is that it can make a difference if it is assumed that an AI program can have emotions, intentions, goals, and values, be aware of them, and can express them – or not.

If a human artist uses an AI program as a tool to generate images, the intention to create art is obviously attributed to the human artist, not to the tool used. But if the AI program is considered to be the author/artist, the situation is different, particularly if the software program used is considered to be the sole author or artist. McCormack et al. raise the non-rhetorical question: how can a software program be considered an 'artist' if it lacks the independent intention to make art or to be an artist?[35]

It can be argued that, in a sense, our definitions of consciousness move in circles. When we define or explain consciousness, or what it means to be conscious of something, we use words like 'ability to feel and experience, having interests and intentions'. These words, in turn, are explained or defined in terms of consciousness, or presuppose a prior understanding of what it means to be conscious. Even so, it is obviously important to separate consciousness and awareness of oneself. The latter is part of our consciousness, but only a subcategory of our conscious experiences.

Walter Glannon clarifies the ethical dimension of consciousness:

> There is a normative ethical dimension to consciousness. This involves questions about the permissibility or impermissibility of actions that alter, suppress, or restore awareness. It also involves questions about how these actions and other events affecting the brain's capacity to generate and sustain awareness can benefit or harm people, as well as judgments about actions performed in altered conscious states.[36]

Attributing awareness and consciousness to some entity or being will therefore have moral implications. Consciousness deserves protection and is valuable. As Glannon puts it, 'For many, the capacity for consciousness is an essential property of being a person.'[37] But this is immediately qualified by Glannon. He argues that consciousness as such does not have intrinsic value. The value of consciousness to a person depends on what it is like for that individual to be aware and what that individual is aware of.

Thus several difficult questions remain to be discussed. By themselves, arousal and awareness have no moral significance. What makes them significant is that they enable us to think, feel, and act. The capacity for consciousness has value when it enables us to adapt to the environment and engage in meaningful mental and physical activities at specific times and over time.[38]

And in his conclusions, Glannon reiterates this point: 'Consciousness as such does not have ethical significance. Being aware is not intrinsically valuable but has value or disvalue depending on the subjective quality and content of our mental states, whether they are pleasurable or painful, and whether it enables us to meaningfully engage with others'.[39]

Machines do not have moral status. They do not deserve our empathy. We do not argue with machines that have broken down or ceased to function properly; we try to repair them. They do not have interests and intentions, and thus they have no interests that we are morally obliged to take into account. That is why the issue of whether it makes sense to say that AI programs have or can develop consciousness is relevant in this context. It may also explain some of the resistance to the idea that AI programs have consciousness. In short, if we assume that at least some AI programs have moral status, they deserve to be treated as persons or sentient beings. This is also a conclusion that some writers have drawn, for instance Philip Galanter.

Generally, we tend to assume that consciousness presupposes the existence of a brain or a central nervous system. An organism without a brain or a nervous system cannot be conscious. This assumption can be checked by a thought experiment developed in detail and discussed by David Chalmers, called 'the philosophical zombie': can we imagine someone behaving exactly like any of us but not having any experiences, thus behaving like an advanced robot? Could I do and say all the things I say and do without being conscious?

According to Galanter, a zombie might make the verbal sounds 'I think, therefore I am', but it will have no awareness of saying it or having said it. He adds: 'Perhaps even the most human-like AIs will be zombies. This poses a serious epistemological challenge in that first-person experience seems to be inaccessible to third persons on the outside looking in. And even if our AIs do have an internal life and are fully sentient, does that necessarily mean we are obliged to view them as patients?'[40]

This thought experiment – the philosophical zombie – has been criticized by Daniel Dennett and others for being impossible; a completely functioning human brain must, by definition, be conscious. Dennett has argued that what David Chalmers has called the hard problem (explaining the relationship between physical processes, such as brain processes, and experience) is not the hard question.[41] But even so, the thought experiment illustrates the difficulty of identifying and isolating behaviour that will indicate with certainty that an organism is conscious.

This can be applied to the present discussion in the following way. Verbal behaviour of an advanced AI software in a particular situation can be very similar to verbal behaviour by a human in the same situation. Nevertheless, it may be difficult to assert or deny with any certainty that this software is conscious or understands what it is saying. This can also be applied to the outcomes of advanced picture-generating AI programs.

Philosophers analysing consciousness have written extensively on the problem: how and why does subjective experience arise from the physical brain? According to Glannon, 'Critical and experiential interests are not biological features but features of a person's conscious mental states. These states depend on but are not reducible to connections between the upper brainstem and thalamus, the thalamus and cortex, and different cortical regions'.[42]

The neurobiology of consciousness is obviously relevant and is discussed in some detail by, among others, Walter Glannon.[43] However, it would carry us too far afield to discuss these aspects of consciousness here.

The philosophy of mind is indeed a vast and complex field in which there are many theories and definitions but little agreement. Existing theories answer the what, how and why questions of consciousness in several ways, according to Robert van Gulik and Walter Glannon.[44] But I will try to limit myself to what is obviously relevant in the present context in a brief exchange of questions and answers.

Question: What could it mean in this context to attribute consciousness to an AI program/software?

Answer/assumption: It would mean that there are AI programs designed in such a way that it makes sense to say that they can have experiences, including being aware to some degree of their intentions, emotions and values. Some of these mental states are often, on somewhat unclear grounds, thought to be specific to humans, such as fear of death and knowing that we are all going to die.

Alternative answer/assumption: AI programs cannot have experiences and intentions of the kinds mentioned in the previous section. Computers are just complex machines. They generate the pictures and information they do because they have been instructed to do so by the software engineer who designed the program. Everything generated by the programs can, in principle, be given a technological explanation.

Comment: At present, there are many known and unknown uncertainties and unknowns concerning these questions. We do not know at present – despite many theories – what consciousness is, where it is located, or its origin. Hence, we are free to make assumptions – if the assumptions are presented as such and not as proven facts. Perhaps we cannot exclude that one day in the future it will make sense to attribute some degree of consciousness to some advanced AI programs.

Question: What would be required for an AI program/software to have consciousness, including awareness of its intentions, emotions and values?

Answer/assumption: Consciousness/awareness, in the relevant sense, would emerge from, or be in some way caused by, non-conscious entities or processes.

Comment: At least for now, there is an explanatory gap indicating an incomplete understanding of how the supposed experiences and intentions of an AI program or software can emerge from something that is not conscious.

Question: What would be the function of the awareness attributed to AI programs/software?

Answer/assumption: If picture-generating AI programs cannot have some minimal degree of awareness of their intentions, emotions and values – including some experiences of past events – they cannot be aware of themselves and of the surrounding world.

Additional answer/assumption: That some AI programs can be aware of themselves and of the surrounding world is necessary for these programs to be able to share experiences, including their intentions, emotions and values, and be able to intend to communicate something about them to others.

3 Same or Different Learning Process?

3.1 Brief Introduction

In this section, some differences between learning processes about art are discussed. The focus is on the comparison between the 'training' of AI programs and young artists. A well-considered answer presupposes some account of different learning processes and a critical examination of analogies between different kinds of such processes.

3.2 The Issue

Another controversial issue concerns the similarities and differences between the 'training' and the 'learning' processes of human artists and picture-generating AI programs:

(2) Are human artists and picture-generating AI programs 'trained' or 'learning' about pictures by others in the same or different way?

When artists create new paintings, they do not start from scratch. They work in a tradition and against a tradition. They borrow and transform. The starting point is pictures by others. In the beginning, works by young artists are imitations and variations of pictures by others. Eventually, young artists find their own voice. Picasso is also an example of this development. His early paintings are close to the prevalent tradition when he started his career and very different from his later ones.

A challenge for teachers in art schools is that there is no recipe for teaching students how to make great art. The art students can be taught about various techniques, about mistakes to be avoided and about the achievements of other artists, but their teachers cannot teach their students to become great artists. They must have certain talents which need to be stimulated and developed. But how? Against this background, it is interesting to check the curriculum of an art institute where young artists are educated. What do they learn and how are they taught?

The Royal Institute of Art in Stockholm describes the courses offered by the Institute on its website. It seems clear that the education is very much concentrated on meeting the needs of the individual student and helping them to find their own voice. The focus is on exploring new knowledge of the expression, methods and contexts of art and architecture. Each art student is given an experienced artist as a supervisor, and together they discuss and agree on the contents of the courses, workshops and seminars the student should participate in.

Knowledge is created in dialogues about changes taking place in art, culture and science. Studio work is combined with courses, workshops, lectures, study trips and exhibitions. The supervisor is responsible for the artistic development of the student. The teachers are highly qualified artists representing different methods and perspectives in order to achieve a broad and deep education.

The importance of an international perspective is stressed. International guest teachers are regularly invited to teach, and international workshops are arranged at the Institute. Study travels abroad are encouraged. The creative artistic work is central at the Institute. New perspectives and contexts are presented during the education in order to facilitate innovative art. The development of an artistic personality is obviously important.

The education at the Institute also includes courses in the history and theory of art. Paintings, sculptures and other works of art are discussed, analysed and interpreted during the education. The students should be familiar with the works of other artists. But this seems very different from the 'learning' and 'training' of picture-generating AI programs, which may be fed thousands of pictures, say from Western art in the last 500 years, along with various labels and/or instructions to make it possible for the program to find patterns in the information it is fed. The precise way in which these learning and teaching processes in art schools and in AI differ from each other is intriguing, also because the technology is in rapid development.

3.3 The Birth of a Work of Art

In the literature on the history of art, there are many descriptions and analyses of processes of creation, sometimes also referring to technical, societal and economic changes during the periods studied. Analyses of the processes involving changes in artistic means of expression are sometimes combined with studies of the biography of the artist. For instance, this is the case in the interpretations of van Gogh's famous self-portrait showing him with a bandage around his head, when he had cut off his ear and given it to a prostitute or cleaner at a brothel.

The more theoretical literature on artistic processes may, at times, focus on the use of pictorial elements based on visual impressions of nature, and sometimes on pictorial elements derived from works of predecessors (Ernst Gombrich, Ragnar Josephson). The latter approach is particularly interesting in the present context. For instance, Gombrich argued for the importance of schemata in analysing works of art.[45] He claimed – and illustrated his claims with many examples – that artists learn to represent the external world by learning from previous artists. Seemingly naturalistic landscape painters have been shown to be using schemata drawn by artists from their predecessors. These pictorial elements, whatever their origin, can be split up, combined, modified, supplemented, regrouped and recombined when an artist working in a tradition but also against a tradition attempts to create something new.

The analyses by Gombrich and Josephson of how pictorial schemata and visual forms are used, from the first sketches to the final work, are primarily applied to representational works of art where artists have worked with sketches. The analyses of how pictorial schemata are used in the creation of artworks are probably more difficult to apply to abstract artworks of the kind created by Per Kirkeby, Torsten Andersson and Barnett Newman.

Sometimes, these creative processes have been combined with personal hardships and sacrifices on the part of the artist; van Gogh is an obvious example. In other cases, fortuitous moments have helped the artist see a possibility to combine different visual forms into something new. A striking example is when Picasso combined the handlebars and saddle of a bicycle into a representation of a bull's head – and the bull, of course, is an important motif in Picasso's art.

Banksy sometimes uses a picture by someone else as a point of departure and changes it by replacing one motif in that picture with another motif. The result can be a picture of a person throwing roses instead of a bomb – a picture expressing a political message. This is very different from the working method of Swedish artist Karin Mamma Andersson, one of the most successful artists of her generation in Sweden. Sometimes she creates art using black and white photos as a point of departure.

Elements in a work of art can be related not only to pictorial elements taken from predecessors. As Jon McCormack et al. remind us, artists can be 'inspired by experience of nature, sounds, relationships, discussions and feelings that a GAN is never exposed to and cannot cognitively process as humans do'.[46] The precise combination of such sources of inspiration can differ from case to case, as a comparison of the works by Turner, Monet, Rothko and Barnett Newman might suggest. They may also differ during different periods in a particular artist's life, as could be illustrated by works created by Gerhard Richter during his long and successful career.

Moreover, photographers like Ansel Adams and Lars Tunbjörk are known to have waited for hours and even days for the right light or the right moment to take a photo. The calculations and hardships during the process have no counterpart in AI programs generating pictures. Artificial intelligence programs do not have to wait for hours and even days for the right light or moment. The difference in time is clear and obvious. How significant is this? What does it show?

Works of art are created in many ways, and the role of the artist, the commissioner and the market has been different during the course of history. There was a time when works of art were commissioned by the church, the nobility or those with money. Well-known case studies include descriptions of the very detailed instructions offered to Perugino by Isabella d'Este for paintings she commissioned.[47] Now works of art are rarely commissioned; they are produced and offered as merchandise on a market for interested buyers. Art is produced in more than one way, and generalizations are difficult.

The precise ways in which these processes of creation differ in art by humans and by picture-generating AI software are intriguing, also because the technology is in rapid development. If, as I would suggest, there are differences (in time, experience required, the way these experiences are processed, and in the hardships involved) between the processes in which pictures are created by humans and by computers, a subsequent question would be whether this is a difference in degree or in kind – and what the significance of these differences is. The significance will, in my view, depend on, and vary with, the assumptions made concerning, in particular, art and creativity.

Summing up so far. During their careers, artists will see many works by other artists and learn from them in developing their own style. Analogously, a picture-generating AI computer program is fed hundreds, and sometimes thousands, of pictures. However, their 'learning processes' are different. In a sense, the computer program is lagging behind and dependent on earlier works by others. The computer program is processing the pictures (or words) it is fed according to the instructions provided by its algorithm. But human learning is based on understanding and experiences and is not mechanical in that way.

Critics and art historians have described the life, education, successes and failures of painters whose works they want to explore, whether it be Dürer, Géricault, van Gogh, Picasso or Rothko. Their studies include analyses of the impulses these artists have received, the influence they have had on others and their personal and artistic achievements. The works of the artists have been analysed and interpreted by being seen and placed in various kinds of contexts, often with the ambition to clarify the growth and development of the work of the particular artists in focus.

The steps in the training of AI software seem very different from the steps in the education of young artists. The thousands of artworks processed by AI software are not related to one particular person's experience, to a particular artistic personality or self, unless we are prepared to assume that the software is that person, is sentient, has consciousness, including experiences and intentions, an assumption discussed in more detail earlier in Section 2.4.

The importance of capacity for experience. Human artists have a capacity for experience. Do computers have such a capacity? Why is a capacity for experience important? Walter Glannon answers this question in the following way: 'The capacity for experience gives us interests in the types of experience we want to have or avoid and grounds explanations for how we can benefit from or be harmed by them. The cognitive, affective, and volitional capacity to make conscious choices and perform intentional and voluntary actions entails taking responsibility and being held responsible for them'.[48]

In any case, learning to produce art requires more than being able to recognize images as images of cats or dogs. Learning involves acquiring understanding, knowledge, skills, values, attitudes and preferences. When humans create art, there is one person who learns by improving his or her technical skills and seeing (and in the beginning, imitating) works by other artists. Artists choose what they want to use, given the values they want to promote, their particular situation and life story.

Implications of the proposed analogy. If there is an analogy between the 'training' and the 'learning' processes of human artists and picture-generating AI programs, this analogy would then suggest that the computer program is to be regarded as the artist, with experiences, interests, a self and a personality. In other words, we are driven back to consider the basic assumptions discussed earlier about the conditions under which it will make sense to attribute experiences and awareness of intentions, emotions and values to computer programs.

The attempt to defend the analogy by recalling how several great names in the history of art often had workshops with many apprentices and others employed does not succeed. It only shows that sometimes many people were involved in the creation of artworks, though the master and owner of the workshop – examples include Rubens and Titian – made the outline and gave the final touch to the work. The impulses from many artists to those that were absorbed in the creation of a particular work need to be distinguished from the many people who sometimes were involved in the process of making the work. It may be helpful to separate the learning process and the execution process; they are different.

AI tools and young artists have different relations to their predecessors. The computer program is 'learning' from an archive of pictures it has been fed, and it works by identifying and extracting patterns in the pictures in this archive. This is done in a mechanical and not subjective way, though the outcome cannot always be predicted, as mentioned earlier. The relation to their predecessors by artists is different. It is based on subjective and not mechanical reactions, learning and accepting some things, but rejecting others. This is done in a process that also involves a fight for attention and recognition, sometimes documented in art manifestos, where differences to the predecessors of the authors are stressed and similarities may be downplayed.

3.4 Anti-technological Attitudes and Thinking Cameras

Blaise Agüera y Arcas discusses the long-standing and complex relationship between art and technology.[49] He draws on Hockney's *Secret Knowledge* for some early examples of artists using optic lenses as tools in painting during the Renaissance, and continues with other examples, including photography. Agüera y Arcas also describes machine learning and the work done by the Google Seattle AI group to explore the potential of using machine intelligence to create art in the Art and Machine Intelligence Program.

In this program, software engineers are working on neurally inspired algorithms based on attempts to approximate the architecture of the brain. Blaise Agüera y Arcas claims that 'Systematically experimenting with what neural-like systems can generate gives us a new tool to investigate nature, culture, ideas, perception, and the workings of our own mind.'[50] In his view, the use of new technologies can have a profound effect on the way we create, think and talk about art.

But he also describes the resistance to applying new technologies to create art, using the history of photography as an illustrative example. In particular, he explores the parallels between resistance to the use of this technology in the past and resistance to the use of computers and machine intelligence in creating art today. For example, it has been suggested that artists using AI technologies are 'cheating', that what they produce is 'kitsch', 'bad art' or not 'real art'.

Creative activities, and in particular art, have appeared to many to be the remaining area of human exceptionalism – an area where humans cannot be replaced by machines. But according to David Gunkel, this may not last much longer. He gives a number of examples of technologies producing what appears to be creative work in music, painting and literature. He concludes that such creative work 'may not be as uniquely human as one might have initially thought'.[51]

Some researchers argue that we should be prepared to abandon the idea of human uniqueness. Philip Galanter is one of them, and Torbjörn Tännsjö seems to be another. Tännsjö makes the point that what is important are the moral implications: our beliefs in the uniqueness and value of our own species.[52] According to Tännsjö, this belief may explain the resistance to the idea that AI programs can have consciousness. He suggests that the idea that we humans are unique is misguided. Thus, what is at stake here is how we perceive ourselves in relation to other living creatures, and Tännsjö claims that we overestimate ourselves and the uniqueness of our mental capabilities.

Agüera y Arcas suggests that the reason for the anti-technological attitudes may well be that the use of these new technologies to create art undermines some deep and old views of what defines us as humans. Concerning what he calls the 'anti-technological concept of art', Agüera y Arcas makes the point that 'if history has anything to teach us in this regard, it is that this particular debate is always ready to resurface'.[53]

Furthermore, he makes the point that some of the art created in this way may be 'beautiful, provocative, frightening, enthralling, unsettling, revelatory, and everything else that good art can be'[54] Hertzmann makes the related suggestion that the use of new AI technologies is likely to have a vitalizing effect on the creation of art. Similar comments have been made by several others in the debate on AI and art, for example by Mazzone and Elgammal, McCormack et al., Chatterjee and Browne.

Blaise Agüera y Arcas supports his criticism of the anti-technological attitude by undermining the sharp distinction between humans and machines: humans use tools, and machines are sometimes programmed to work like neural networks. He states that technologies have always affected art. He mentions as examples the invention of applied pigments, the printing press, photography, computers and AI. Machado Oliveira also criticizes the alleged opposition between humans and machines. The human and the machine should not be put in opposition; a key premise in her article on future imaginings in art and AI is 'the possibility and desirability of conceiving of the human-machine relation without opposition between the two terms'.[55]

Agüera y Arcas approvingly discusses views that invite us to rethink art as something that is generated and consumed by hybrid beings. Moreover, he makes the bold statement that cameras are 'thinking machines'.[56] This claim deserves some comments. Does it follow that to support criticism of the anti-technological attitude, we have to ascribe mental capacities to machines?

The bold statement in previous paragraph is, in my view, very problematic. He makes the point that digital cameras are 'powered by software, amounting at a minimum to millions of lines of code'. He describes in some detail the functions of these codes. Blaise Agüera y Arcas concludes that the 'images we see can only be "beautiful" or "real-looking" because they have been heavily processed', and that in the case of the software, 'this processing relies on the norms and aesthetic judgments on the part of software engineers'. Therefore, 'there is no such thing as a natural image'.[57]

So far, so good. But it does not follow from the statement that digital cameras have been programmed by software engineers that these cameras program themselves, or that we need to attribute mental capacities to cameras, to assume that they can think, have experiences and intentions.

4 Same or Different Creative Process?

4.1 Introduction

In this section, I will comment on two analyses of different kinds of creativity. The distinction between creativity and variations on a well-known theme is discussed, followed by some examples of creative problem-solving in the visual arts. Having done that, some borderline cases, underlying assumptions and other problems are identified and discussed briefly.

4.2 The Issue

The controversies raised by the use of AI programs to make images concern several interrelated issues, including:

(3) Do computers, and in particular advanced AI programs like AICAN, create like humans?

A well-considered answer to this question presupposes some account of how humans create art. Accounts and case studies by critics and art historians exist. They can be used for the comparison suggested in question (3).

Creativity is important in many areas: in scientific work, in human relations, in engineering and indeed in almost any conceivable area of human endeavour. Creativity in art is a special case of creativity in general, on which there is a large literature to which philosophers, economists, psychologists, social scientists and art historians have contributed.

Artistic activity is indeed often considered to be the obvious and prime example of creative activity. In this section, I will take a brief look at some analyses of and assumptions about creativity in art. In the light of these assumptions, I will then compare pictures created by humans and by AI programs. To minimize generalities, I will focus on the visual arts. As mentioned earlier, other art forms such as music, literature, or theatre may raise special issues. Discussing them would require more space than is available here.

How many kinds of creativity? 'Creative' and 'creativity' are words used in many different contexts, and more than one analysis of the concept may be called for. The analysis proposed by Nils-Eric Sahlin has some similarities to the analysis by Margaret Boden,[58] but there are also several interesting differences. The starting point for both is that ideas are the primary entities to which creativity is attributed. According to Boden, a creative idea is new, surprising and valuable. Sahlin specifies in what way the creative idea is valuable: by solving or shedding light on a problem. Boden expresses herself more generally and makes the point that relevant values can vary depending on area; they may also be short-term or long-term.

Boden distinguishes between three kinds of creativity: combinational, exploratory and transformational. 'Accepted style of thinking or conceptual space' are key concepts in the analysis of the latter two, which are close to what Sahlin calls concept-creativity and rule creativity.[59] 'Conceptual space' includes scientific theories and games. But it seems important to distinguish between, for instance, rules defining the game of chess and rules for how to make an impressionist painting. The latter can be vague and interpreted in somewhat different ways compared to the rules defining the game of chess. Moreover, the rules defining the game of tennis are different from the style of playing tennis.

The first of the three kinds of creativity – combinational creativity – is characterized by Boden as involving 'making unfamiliar combinations of familiar ideas',[60] 'the generation of unfamiliar (and interesting) combinations of familiar ideas'[61] or 'the unfamiliar juxtaposition of familiar ideas'.[62] If this is interpreted in an abstract way and in general terms, a problem could be that this kind of creativity ends up as a version of what Sahlin calls rule or concept-creativity. If, on the other hand, one were to take a close look at the examples of *combinational* creativity that are described in the works by Josephson and Gombrich,[63] one might be tempted to look for several subtypes. The focus could be not only on combining ideas and pictorial elements in unfamiliar ways but also on separating and eliminating some ideas or pictorial elements.

A basic distinction. Nils-Eric Sahlin illustrates, with examples from the history of science, how we are prisoners of theoretical systems where there is agreement on rules to be followed and on interpretations of key concepts.[64] He distinguishes two basic forms of creativity: rule creativity and conceptual creativity,[65] two sides of the same coin, as Sahlin later stresses.[66] Creativity, in his view, involves breaking of rules or changes of concepts in order to solve or shed light on problems. Variations are possible depending on what rules are broken, how they are broken, and how basic the rules are.

Artists making impressionist paintings today can produce beautiful and technically skilful works, but in Sahlin's view, they are hardly creative.[67] They make variations on a well-known theme; they remain within a well-established framework of rules for how an impressionist painting should be made. Sahlin contrasts such variations on a well-established theme with the work by Dan Wolgers, a well-known Swedish artist who breaks rules – not for its own sake but to generate new questions and perspectives, to solve problems, for instance regarding our views on art and the role of the artist – including who should be in aesthetic control of an exhibition.

As an example, Sahlin presents the following case.[68] Dan Wolgers is contacted by a gallery, and offered the possibility to exhibit his works in that gallery. The artist accepts the invitation but says that he will not arrange the exhibition himself. He will ask a Public Relations agency to make the selection of his works but promises that he will attend the opening. Here, some basic rules about how exhibitions are arranged, and in particular about the role of artists in arranging exhibitions at galleries, are broken.

Creativity, traditions and time. Artists work in a tradition but also against a tradition, as already mentioned. A work of art, such as a sculpture, needs to resemble earlier works in some ways in order to be perceived as a work in that genre (sculpture). But it also has to deviate in some ways. If it does not, it will be regarded as plagiarism and its creator as an epigon. But if it deviates in every respect from works in the current traditions, it will be unintelligible. An installation in the days of Rembrandt or Vermeer would have been bewildering; spectators would be at a complete loss; they would not know how to deal with it.

This has the implication that there is an important difference between, for instance, the paintings Picasso and Braque made around 1908 and any similar painting made today. These early paintings mark the beginning of cubism and clearly meet the conditions for creativity. But very similar paintings made today do not. They are variations on a well-known theme. However, they may very well have considerable aesthetic value.

More examples of creative problem-solving in the arts. I agree with the important distinction between variations on a well-known theme and creativity as the breaking of rules to solve or shed light on a problem, as proposed by Sahlin. With the benefit of hindsight, we can see today that the ready-mades exhibited by Marcel Duchamp and Andy Warhol paved the way for new forms of art, conceptual art, based on and promoting appreciation of new (cognitive) values in art.

It can be argued that this is also true of some of Damien Hirst's best-known spectacular works, still embattled.[69] They include a tiger shark floating in a giant formaldehyde-filled tank, entitled *The Physical Impossibility of Death in the Mind of Somebody Living* and *Mother and Child Divided*. The latter is a floor-based sculpture or installation comprising four glass-walled tanks containing the two halves of a cow and calf.

Summing up: creative and traditional problem-solving. To sum up, drawing on the work by Sahlin on creativity, we may single out what he regards as genuine creativity, essentially characterized by breaking rules and using new methods and tools to solve problems, whereas traditional problem-solving consists in using established methods and well-known tools to solve or shed light on problems. John Cage's composition *4′33″* is an obvious example of the former, while artists painting today in impressionist style represent the latter.

4.3 Some Problems

Creativity, choices and values. When Tunbjörk, Adams and other photographers wait for hours and even days for the right light to take a picture, they make a choice between different possibilities, and the choice they make is in order to promote certain values and combinations of values. Their choices are related to values, in other words.

Is there a choice between possibilities? If so, who makes it? Choices to promote certain values are, in my view, not made by AI programs generating pictures. The program certainly does not wait for the right light for hours and days; it rapidly produces a number of pictures as instructed directly or indirectly by the algorithm created by the software designer. The word 'right' before 'light' in the previous sentence is not innocent; it carries a heavy burden of knowledge of the effects of different conditions of light and of normative artistic ideals or goals to be achieved.

The software engineer may appear to be a more plausible candidate than the AI program. But that would presuppose that the engineer was aware of the different possibilities, that is, how a particular motif, such as a landscape, would appear in various kinds of light and how that would affect the photos taken – as well as the extent to which photos taken under various conditions of light would exhibit or promote certain values or combinations of values. In other words, the engineer would have all the talents and competencies of the artist, in this case, the photographer. Theoretically, this is not impossible, but it is extremely unlikely.

But suppose the user masters the technology and knows what the result will be after a number of iterations (a difficulty that should not be underestimated in view of the lack of transparency of the program). Then the technology becomes a tool for the user, and he or she makes the choice. This is also the case if the users select among the pictures produced by the AI program those that, in their view, will promote or exhibit the particular combination of values the users are looking for.

Creativity within variations on a well-known theme? One could ask if it would not be possible to talk about creativity also in a somewhat attenuated sense – in some cases that are variations on a well-known theme. Consider, for instance, the still lifes by Cezanne or the many versions he painted of Mont Sainte-Victoire. In the still lifes, he varied a well-known theme, but many art historians and critics, for instance, Roger Fry,[70] would no doubt be prepared to say that he did so in a new and original way.

Comparisons between creativity by humans and by AI can be developed in several ways. The distinction between creativity and variations on a well-known theme is relevant to the present discussion, since, prima facie, one might be inclined to say that computer programs cannot be creative in the senses discussed by Sahlin. But AI programs may certainly – like artists working in a tradition – be able to combine well-known pictorial elements and schemata in new, beautiful and surprising ways.

Creativity, intentions and consciousness. Boden asks: 'Why then is it so widely believed that creativity requires consciousness?' She answers as follows: 'The reason, I suggest, is that many of the creative activities of adults … are consciously monitored throughout, sometimes in a highly self-conscious way … they typically involve a conscious judgment that the final idea is valuable.'[71]

This is close to what Sahlin writes about creativity as goal-directed behaviour.[72] If creative discoveries do not arise by coincidence or happy chance, but require some goal-directed activity, as Sahlin proposes, we must be prepared to assume that computer programs can have or exhibit goal-directed activities in order to argue that computer programs can be creative. Analogously, for the suggestion made by Boden, we must be prepared to assume that computer programs typically can somehow involve a conscious judgement that the final idea is valuable. Both answers raise a problem.

How could disagreements about such assumptions be settled? Can a certain activity and its outcome be interpreted both as goal-directed and as a result of randomness? What is required to make sure that the activity is goal-directed? An intention to achieve a particular goal is certainly required. Randomness or happy coincidences can help, but creativity requires an intention or will to solve a problem, according to Sahlin.[73]

What in AI-generated images would correspond to rule- and concept-creativity, if intentions to solve or shed light on a problem are required? It seems that we would have to be prepared to assume that the AI software used is aware and conscious, so that it makes sense to attribute goal-directed activities to this software. Thus, we are driven back to consider some of the basic assumptions about the origin and location of consciousness (that someone or something is aware of its emotions, values, plans, what it wants to achieve and avoid – at least to some minimal degree) as discussed earlier.

Suppose that (only) thoughts or ideas can be creative, as both Sahlin and Boden suggest, and that we are prepared to assume that computer programs can be creative. Then we must also assume that computer programs have ideas. What would this require? Here, we are again driven back to consider some basic philosophical and scientific theories about the origin, location and function of consciousness, questions on which there is little agreement.

Boden discusses in some detail controversies related to theories about consciousness.[74] Her conclusion is that consciousness and some other key concepts like 'intentionality' are so controversial and poorly understood that it would be premature at present to answer the question of whether creativity and AI is a contradiction in terms.

4.4 A Tentative Conclusion

Those who answer the question discussed in this section ('Do computers create like humans?') in the negative, like Mazzone and Elgammal, are in my view right. Computers do not create like humans.

But their reason for their negative answer is different from mine. They give a technical reason: the computer has failed to imitate the pictures it has been fed. That is why the faces in the AI-generated pictures look like distorted portraits by Francis Bacon. But the difference is that there is no intention (on the part of the program) involved.

My reasons for a negative answer are different. Mazzone and Elgammal focus on the outcome of the process of creation, whereas I focus on the underlying assumptions about the value dimensions of art and on the differences between the kind of problem-solving that artists and AI are involved in. These differences will be explored in the next section.

5 Same or Different Kinds of Thinking?

5.1 Introduction

In this section, I begin by outlining briefly two kinds of thinking and problem-solving at which AI excels: analytical and instrumental thinking. Another kind of thinking, critical thinking, that is important in philosophy and in scientific research is also described briefly. They are contrasted with two kinds of thinking, important to us as humans and arguably to human artists in their work, hermeneutic and empathic thinking.

5.2 The Issue

Another controversial and interrelated issue concerns differences between problems and problem-solving in art and AI. The issue can be stated as follows:

(4) Are picture-generating AI-programs capable of the sort of thinking and understanding required for the creation of art?

or

(4)' Is the kind of information processing and problem-solving at which AI excels of any use or relevance in creating art?

A well-considered answer presupposes some account of different kinds of thinking and problem-solving inside and outside of the realm of art, including an account of the sort of thinking and understanding required to create art.

Obviously, there are several kinds of problems and ways of solving them. Distinctions between a few of them are relevant also for those who want to take a position on some of the issues raised by the use of AI to create images. In addition to the different creative processes and the previously discussed dubious analogy between how artists are educated in art schools and how AI programs are 'trained', a consideration of these differences is important for those who want to take a position on whether computers can create art.

5.3 Five Kinds of Thinking

Artificial intelligence tools are used in many areas today. For instance, there are obvious possibilities in finding patterns in diagnostic images of breast cancer, in the planning of healthcare, and dealing with logistic challenges raised by traffic on roads and rails. Here are some examples of what AI can contribute:

Analytic thinking. An AI computer program can analyse large amounts of data and find patterns in them, for instance in planning where, when and what type of healthcare services should be provided, based on correlations between different variables such as age, diagnosis, contact with healthcare, treatment, costs, results, follow-up and rehabilitation. Artificial intelligence can do this faster and more accurately than a human being is able to. The patterns found can then be used for planning, prediction and control.

Instrumental thinking. Suppose the task is to find the shortest, fastest, cheapest way to achieve a particular specified goal. If the computer is programmed with precise instructions that clarify the goal, the present position, distance from there to the goal, possible obstacles on the road as well as ways to reduce, eliminate or circumvent the obstacles, then tasks of this kind can be solved quickly and accurately by an AI computer program.

The two kinds of thinking outlined in the previous paragraphs illustrate somewhat different kinds of information processing. Here, AI is being used successfully in many areas, but there are other forms of thinking and problem-solving. The complexity of the human brain compared to the computer – which can be measured and graded – is not the decisive factor. The distinction between different kinds of thinking is more important. Other forms of thinking and problem-solving include but are not limited to:

Hermeneutic thinking. Humans are confronted with situations and problems that, in order to be solved or dealt with, require interpretation and understanding; the meaning and significance of signs and situations have to be interpreted and understood. Only then can these problems be dealt with in a satisfactory way. Existential problems – raised by suffering, sorrow, loneliness and the death of loved persons – belong to this category. Such problems are often the subject matter in works of art.

Empathetic thinking. This kind of thinking is essential in relation to care and care ethics. It requires the ability to put yourself in the situation of other people and to imagine living in their world. Søren Kierkegaard once wrote that to be able to reach and influence other human beings, you must first move yourself to where they are. This presupposes some kind of empathy, a term with several meanings, ranging from psychological ability to imagine oneself in the situation of others to acting selflessly, as Mats Johansson has shown.[75]

In cognitive research and philosophy, other forms of thinking are discussed and analysed, for instance, critical thinking. The task is then to identify the assumptions a line of thought or reasoning presupposes, to examine the evidence available pro and con these assumptions, to find knowledge gaps and uncertainties, as well as missing value premises. This includes critical examination of, and reflection on, one's own values, as well as knowing what one does not know, as Sahlin emphasizes.[76]

But completeness is not an end in itself in this context. The purpose of these distinctions is only to give examples of different kinds of thinking relevant for the discussion of the use of AI in creating art. The point of the distinctions between different kinds of thinking is this: adherents and critics may agree that AI has come to stay when the problem requires certain forms of reliable and fast information processing, illustrated by the first two ways of thinking. But AI is not helpful in situations which presuppose interpretation and understanding of situations, persons, actions or material, including texts.

The last two forms of thinking and problem-solving are relevant for artistic creation and some of the values works of art may possess or promote. Perhaps this can at least partly be summed up in what may look like a catchword: to show what it means to be a human being today. This is something that is rendered in visual form by a human being with a certain life history and experience (the artist) and is interpreted by people with other experiences and life histories (the spectators).

The view of human beings and the human condition conveyed by the sculptures of Giacometti (or the plays of Samuel Beckett, to take an example from literature) is not arrived at by analysing large sets of data and finding patterns in them on the basis of correlations between variables. Hermeneutic and empathic thinking is required as well as technical skill. A glance at the history of sculpture from Michelangelo to Brancusi and Giacometti is instructive and can provide further food for thought.

When Giacometti and others create art, I will argue that they use hermeneutic and empathic thinking, and use their technical skills to promote, enhance or achieve certain values. These values will be described in some detail in the next section. Thus, I want to argue that the kind of thinking described here under the subheading 'analytic thinking' is not what is relevant when humans create art.

If hermeneutic and empathic thinking are essential in the arts and for us as humans, then this difference in thinking points to a problem concerning the possibility of computer programs to create art. Computer programs cannot feel pain or loss, nor sorrow at the death of a loved one. Nor can they interpret and understand the pain and sorrow of others. But whether this problem can be overcome also requires a discussion of criteria and conditions of art. There is a difference between seeking novel modes of expression and finding patterns in works produced by others. Pictures created by AI using the analytic thinking described earlier in this section can be missing in depth, lacking a human dimension, but they may still be interesting to look at. The visual shapes or forms can be surprising and intriguing. But is it art? This is the focus of the next section.

5.4 A Tentative Conclusion

The five kinds of thinking described here serve different kinds of interests, only some of which are, in my view, relevant to the creation of art. Hermeneutical and empathic thinking are related to human activities and the interest of orienting action and reaching understanding, and sometimes also in emancipation and in promoting autonomy and responsibility. These interests can be found exemplified also in the arts, in combination with interests to promote certain values that are examined in what follows.

Is there a ghost in the machine? There may be more important issues to worry about, such as whether 'humans as primitive robots in this new foreign landscape can find a new orientation and vision for the human condition'.[77] But, nevertheless, we could ask: does it make sense to suggest that there is an artificial self in a software that produces outcomes that the programmer did not anticipate, as they were not part of the programming?

AI technology is developing with such rapidity that the kinds of thinking discussed in this section make no claim of completeness. New AI tools may explore and be based on combinations of thinking not discussed here. It should be kept in mind that the list of AI tools is long, and new additions to the list continue to be made with applications in many areas (including also language, music and pictures).

For instance, there are now tools that can make concise summaries of long and complex texts. Recent tools include ChatGPT4 and Google Bard. Such AI tools are neither good nor bad, with a possible exception for some military tools, like AI-Controlled Killer Drones. However, many AI tools can be put to good uses as well as to those that are morally unacceptable. Tools for facial recognition illustrate this point. As for responsibility issues, there is an important distinction between using AI tools as decision aids and letting AI tools make the decisions.

Can everything that happens when AI programs are generating new pictures be given a technological explanation? This is not easy to say, given the lack of transparency concerning what goes on in the more advanced AI software. We may then have to argue hypothetically and say: if there are AI programs producing new and original pictures, then perhaps computers can create art, provided that certain assumptions about art are accepted. These assumptions will be discussed in the next section.

6 Is It Art?

6.1 Introduction

The controversy to be discussed in this section, sparked by events published in media, is perhaps the one that has attracted the most attention:

(5) Can computers create art?

It is also complex and difficult, since many issues are involved, and possible answers are based on assumptions that need to be made explicit and argued for.

In this section, the focus will be on the various kinds of values that works of art can have or promote. A well-considered answer presupposes some criteria or definition of art. This is a subject on which there is a very extensive literature.[78] I will argue that hypothetical answers to question (5) and its variants are needed, and illustrate this need with an example and then suggest some tentative conclusions.

6.2 The Issues

To begin, some preliminary distinctions between different issues need to be made. The focus in the discussion of the general question (5) can be on the result or on the process. If the focus is on the result, the general issue can be rephrased as:

(5.1) Can pictures – or other works – generated by AI tools, such as Midjourney, DreamWorks or AICAN, be art? What would be required for this to happen?

This question captures the value dimensions of 'art'. The answer to this question will depend on what assumptions one is prepared to make and defend concerning art, whether the computer programs used are or can be sentient, autonomous, have intentions, and to some minimal degree at least be aware of what they are doing.

But the general question (5) can also be interpreted in ways that can be investigated empirically:

(5.2) Will the AI tools used to generate pictures or other works ever be widely credited as authors of artworks by the general public? What would this require?

or

(5.3) Will pictures or works generated by AI tools ever be widely considered as works of art by the general public? What would this require?

Here, 'the general public' can be replaced by specific descriptions of different publics, including 'the art world'.

If, however, the focus is on the process and the answer to the general question (5) is affirmative, then this question can be replaced by:

(5.4) Are computer programs tools for human artists, but not artists, or are the computer programs artists and not just tools for human artists? What would this require?

The answer to this question will also depend on the assumptions one is prepared to make concerning the possibilities of the technology, the values that works of art can have or promote, and whether the programs are or can be sentient, autonomous, have intentions and to some minimal degree at least be aware of what they are doing.

I will return to these issues and answer them tentatively at the end of this section.

6.3 Empirical Approaches

The Turing test. It may be tempting to use the outcome of some variant of a Turing test to decide if spectators can distinguish between AI-generated works and works generated by human artists – and hence to decide if at least some AI-produced pictures are works of art, or deserve to be called art.

Margaret Boden writes that for an artistic program to pass the Turing test would 'be for it to produce artwork which was (1) indistinguishable from one produced by a human being, and/or (2) was seen as having as much aesthetic value as one produced by a human being'.[79]

She adds that with regard to the second criterion, it would count as passing the test even if the machine's performance was 'comparable only to relatively mediocre human art'.[80] The last part of the quotation contains several vague words that may make it difficult to settle disagreement as to whether the test has been passed.

Boden has argued that many works generated by AI 'strongly' pass the Turing test. She concludes her article by writing that the Turing test has been passed 'behaviourally' already – 'occasionally, at a world class level. Where non-interactive examples (such as AARON and Emmy) are concerned, the test has been passed in a relatively strong form'.[81] Here there is a problem. Who is deciding whether the two conditions are met? If the decision is made by other human beings, we need to know the principles for the selection of the judges and the relevance of their verdicts.

Mazzone and Elgammal have also carried out empirical research, which they summarize as follows:

> We devised a visual Turing test to register how people would react to the generated images and whether they could tell the difference between AICAN- or human-created art. To make the test timely and of high quality, we mixed images from AICAN with works from Art Basel 2016. . . . We also used a set of images from abstract expressionist masters as a baseline. Our study showed that human subjects could not tell whether the art was made by a human artist or by the machine. Seventy-five percent of the time, people in our study thought that the AICAN generated images were created by a human artist. In the case of the baseline abstract expressionist set, 85% of the time subjects thought that the art was by human artists.[82]

Surveys. Is it plausible to assume that the general public at art exhibitions recognize pictures produced by AI tools as art and appreciate their aesthetic and artistic qualities? This has, in fact, been investigated by Mazzone and Elgammal. They describe the aim of their empirical survey as follows: 'to gauge whether the AICAN works were aesthetically recognizable as art, and whether human viewers liked the AI-generated works of art'.[83]

By using 'art' and 'works of art' rather than 'pictures', the authors beg the question of whether these pictures are indeed works of art.

Other more recent empirical studies have been made. For instance, Andrew Samo and Scott Highhouse found that 'participants were able to successfully classify the images as human- or machine-generated art 60% of the time. The classification accuracy was higher for human images at 85% and lower for machine images at 35%'.[84] They also found that the participants preferred human-generated art over machine-generated art. Boden reports similar findings: 'Sometimes, on discovering that the image/music they had previously admired was generated by a computer, people simply withdraw their previous valuation.'[85]

There is a fundamental problem with any empirical approaches, including empirical tests and surveys. These approaches will answer empirical questions like 'Are pictures generated by certain AI programs regarded as art by certain groups of visitors?' or 'Can visitors always distinguish between works created by human artists and pictures generated by certain AI programs?' But they will not solve the problem (5), since art is a value-loaded concept. The question of whether pictures generated by AI tools are works of art is partly about whether these pictures deserve to be called art or ought to be regarded as art.

6.4 Assumptions about Art and Values

Points of departure. Value is a difficult concept; there are many kinds of value, and it is far from clear how they are related to each other. Moreover, the key terms in this section, 'artistic' and 'aesthetic', can be interpreted in many ways. What Berys Gaut has called the cluster account of art is a useful point of departure in the present context,[86] although I do not want to rule out the possibility of a disjunctive definition of art. His central idea is that art is a cluster concept in the sense that one can give a set of criteria,

> satisfaction of which counts towards something being art, but which need not all be satisfied for something to count as art. These criteria, I have argued, include such things as being beautiful (or possessing other narrow aesthetic properties), being expressive of emotion, being intellectually challenging, being formally complex and coherent, having the capacity to convey complex meanings, exhibiting an individual point of view, being an exercise of creative imagination, being the product of a high degree of skill, belonging to an established artistic form and being the product of an art-making intention.[87]

It seems that many of these proposed criteria refer to various kinds of value. In what I once called the Umbrella theory of art, I argued that there is a plurality of aesthetic, artistic, cognitive and other values that artworks can have or promote (in addition to their possible historical, therapeutic and economic value).[88] These values can be graded and combined in different ways in works of art, and we cannot assume that there is just one criterion or art-making property that in all cultures and at all times will single out what is art.

Relations between values. How are the values discussed in this section related to each other more precisely? To answer this question, a detailed analysis of the key concepts or a theory of art would be needed. Many such theories have been proposed in the course of history, from Plato and Kant to George Dickie, but no universal agreement on these theories has been achieved. Part of the problem – as has been noted in the debate – is (a) that there is a variety of aesthetic qualities, not just the traditional categories beautiful and ugly, (b) that not all aesthetic terms referring to such qualities are evaluative, and (c) that several aesthetic terms are used also outside the area of art criticism. In the present context, it is enough to argue that if the values differ in some respect, they cannot be identified.

Both the cluster account of art and the Umbrella theory are alternatives to the sociological institutional theory of art, which can be summarized in statements like, 'art is what the art world considers to be art' and 'Good art is what the art world considers to be good art'.[89] The Umbrella theory is based on the assumptions: (1) that 'art' is a positively value-loaded term, although 'bad art' is not a contradiction in terms; (2) that controversies over what is art and good art concern the values that art can have or promote – rather than the actions of the agents of the art world (such as critics, curators, gallery owners); and (3) that these values can be defined and combined in different ways, which explains why the general umbrella of art covers so many different items and activities.

The Umbrella theory tries to make explicit the value component of art. What is important is not the activities and actions by the agents in the art world, but the reasons for their actions. Values play an important role in this context.

There are several kinds of values that are relevant in this text. They will be explained briefly in the following and are summarized in a brief list, indicating possible assumptions about AI-generated pictures:

AI-generated pictures can have, or promote, aesthetic value
AI-generated pictures can have, or promote, artistic value
AI-generated pictures can have, or promote, cognitive value
AI-generated pictures can have, or promote, economic value
AI-generated pictures can have, or promote, therapeutic value
AI-generated pictures can have, or promote, historic value

These statements can be joined by 'and/or'. Each of the values on this list can be defined in more than one way. Moreover, this list of values makes no claim to completeness. In addition to these values, there are also moral values that at times play a controversial role in the evaluation of art. These moral values may be combined with aesthetic, artistic and other values, but it is not difficult to find examples in the history of art criticism of conflicts between moral and other values of art.

The first three of these values in the list will now be briefly characterized in the next section; the others will be discussed in a following section.

6.5 Key Values

Aesthetic value. Philosophers have developed theories of beauty using as a starting point somewhat vague conceptions of beauty like 'a combination of qualities, such as shape, colour, or form, that pleases the senses, especially the sight'. This has also been the basis for more practical applications in art schools and beauty clinics.

This idea has been developed by philosophers in different ways. There are considerable variations in the way 'aesthetic value' is used. Some use 'aesthetic value' to refer to appearances; others use it to refer to some specific conception of beauty (presumably definable in terms of harmony, elegance, balance, etc.) of what they perceive. If 'aesthetic value' involves cognition and interpretation, the distinction between aesthetic and some other kinds of value becomes less clear.

The central aesthetic value, beauty in classical aesthetics, is in this context based on the idea that everything in a work is in its right place. Nothing can be added, moved or deleted without making the work less beautiful, less aesthetically satisfying. In minimalist aesthetics, the aim is to remove everything from a picture that is not necessary.

Empirical research has been carried out by Daniel Berlyne and others to identify visual patterns that are considered aesthetically satisfying in different cultures.[90]

In the aesthetic literature, there are theories about aesthetic objects, aesthetic experiences, aesthetic attitudes, and aesthetic judgements. But these theories have lost some of their appeal since developments within the arts in the last hundred years have demonstrated that not all art is beautiful and that not everything that is beautiful is art. These theoretical issues will not be explored further here. Instead, the focus will be on more practical and empirical aspects indicated in the previous and the next paragraph.

Can the aesthetic value of a work be examined intersubjectively and empirically? The aesthetic value of a work can be checked by practical tests, by adding something, by covering or changing any part of the work to see whether this adds to or detracts from the value of the work. Such practical tests can, in principle, be applied to works in any style, from any time or culture, including *The Three Musicians* by Picasso, *View from Delft* by Vermeer, as well as *Six Persimmons* by Mu Chi. The outcome of the test may be, for instance, that the work will be better if a certain part of it is deleted. Depending on the reasons given for the outcome of the test, the aesthetic value may be more or less closely related to the artistic and cognitive value of the work.

Suppose aesthetic value is an important value in (some) art. Does it make sense to assume that AI programs can generate pictures with considerable aesthetic value? It does, and there is empirical evidence for this. Many AI-generated pictures have striking aesthetic qualities. But this does not require that we assume that AI programs generating these pictures have conscious and/or subconscious experiences and intentions. Sunsets and landscapes like the Grand Canyon in the United States can be breathtaking and have aesthetic value, but they are not works of art; they are not created by humans and do not want to communicate, share or express anything. The Grand Canyon is not about anything; it is not an intentional object.

Artistic value. It is essential to separate artistic from aesthetic value. Unfortunately, there are and have been many different ideas about how to define artistic value. A proposal that, for some time, had many followers was the idea made popular by Leo Tolstoy that the key is the capacity of a work of art to express and communicate feelings.[91]

But a dominating idea concerning artistic value in our time and culture is that originality is a central aspect. This idea is not very old; it can be traced back to Romanticism, and in particular to Edward Young's *Conjectures on Original Composition*, 1759. The idea is thus rather new in the long history of art; originality has not always been a central artistic value. Technical skill has, in many cultures, including ours, been regarded as an important value.

Suppose originality is an important artistic value. Does this require that we assume that the artist has conscious and/or subconscious experiences and intentions? It depends to some extent on how originality is defined. Suppose that the visual shape of an AI-generated picture is new and original in the sense that a picture with this precise visual shape has never before existed. Therefore, it surprises the user of the program as well as the art public. Even so, there is no need to attribute experiences and intentions to the program.

However, there are other ideas of what constitutes artistic value. An interesting idea suggested by the art critic John Berger[92] is this: an artist has seen or experienced something which he or she has managed to render in such a way that the work acquires a life of its own. It carries on a dialogue with the artist during the creative work and later on with spectators from different times and places:

'When a painting is lifeless it is the result of the painter not having the nerve to get close enough for a collaboration to start. He stays at a *copying* distance.'[93] A few pages later, Berger adds, 'And when the painted image is not a copy but the result of a dialogue, the painted thing speaks if we listen'.[94]

According to Berger, when such collaboration has taken place and is understood, it offers us an insight as to why we are moved by the painting. But what is required for this dialogue to be possible? This remains to be clarified.

By developing Kant's aesthetics, Paul Crowther has suggested a somewhat different interpretation of artistic originality,[95] based on the idea that an original work presents a way of seeing the world that has not been done before. He argues that

> a work's individuality can refine or innovate in relation to the scope of its medium. When this occurs (...) the work can have an objective value which representations that merely repeat established patterns and formulae of production do not. By virtue of its *creative difference* from other representations, it opens up new possibilities of aesthetic experience. *This is the basis of an authentic canon of major works and artists or creative ensembles.*[96]

Later on the same page, Crowther adds, 'By developing the logical possibilities of a medium, the artist opens up new ways of presenting the world.'

If this is the point of departure, it seems difficult to escape the implication that it presupposes that the artist had experiences and intentions to present these experiences visually in a novel way. Thus, if an AI program generating pictures is to be regarded as an artist, it seems to require – on this latter conception of originality as an artistic value – that it makes sense to say that the program can have experiences and intentions.

According to the previous conception of artistic value, the key idea is that the artistic value of a work of art implies that the work presents a new way of looking at the world. A different but somewhat related idea implies that the work presents a new way of looking at art, a new conception of what art is. In *Beyond the Brillo Box*, Arthur Danto argues that Warhol's *Brillo Box* 1964 has changed the way art is made, perceived, and exhibited. The artistic value of a work is then related to its position in the history of art. As also some of Duchamp's ready-mades show, this does not require that the artist created the work, or that it has aesthetic value. As a matter of fact, some conceptual artworks have no aesthetic properties at all but consist of an idea, presented in a fax or by social media.

Cognitive value. In general terms, cognitive value can be defined as follows according to Elisabeth Schellekens: 'By cognitive value, what is meant is simply the value an artwork may have in virtue of enhancing or increasing our understanding of some topic, notion or event.'[97] Aesthetic and cognitive value may very well be combined: 'A work's aesthetic value may well strengthen and intensify its cognitive value, and vice versa.'[98] We see movies, read novels, regard paintings not only to pass time or be entertained but to better understand the world in which we are living.

Paul Klee emphasizes the cognitive value of art in his famous remark: 'Art does not render the visible, but it makes visible.'[99] Art can provide new insights, new perspectives, raise new questions and stimulate new thoughts and considerations. There are several ways in which this can be achieved: a work can present a metaphor or an analogy that makes us notice something we otherwise had missed. In other cases, we may draw conclusions about events or processes from what is presented or depicted in a work; in still others, we may draw conclusions about the artist and his or her mental state when a particular work was created. These variations are based on assumptions or conventions used when artworks are interpreted.

Suppose cognitive value is an important value in (at least some) art. Does it make sense to assume that AI programs can generate pictures with considerable cognitive value? It will depend on the exact definition of 'cognitive value' and on the assumptions governing the interpretation of the picture. But it would seem reasonable to suppose that at least some AI-generated pictures can have cognitive qualities; they can raise new questions, make us reconsider choices we made, reveal aspects of notions or events that we might have missed otherwise. But this does not require that we assume that the AI program generating these pictures has conscious and subconscious experiences and intentions.

If AI-generated pictures enhance or increase our understanding of some topic, notion or event, because *we* read something into them, we do not have to attribute experiences and intentions to the AI program generating the pictures. If, however, we assume that the pictures are based on some experiences and made with the intention to increase or enhance our understanding of some topic or event, the situation will obviously be different. There are also differences in this respect between different art forms, such as poetry, movies, music, painting, and theatre plays, which cannot be explored here.

6.6 Other Values

Moral values. There are individuals and groups among critics, art historians and aestheticians who argue that moral values are irrelevant in the evaluation of art. For instance, the formalist camp, with Clive Bell and Roger Fry, advocated such views. Moreover, as is well known, Oscar Wilde, apparently defending a version of the autonomy of art doctrine in *The Picture of Dorian Gray* wrote: 'There's no such thing as a moral or an immoral book, books are well written or badly written, that is all.'

The relation between moral and aesthetic values is a very complex topic, thoroughly analyzed in detail by Berys Gaut.[100] It would require more space than is available here to pursue this topic. Having said this, I am aware of the oversimplification in the formalist views – also illustrated by the famous quotation from Oscar Wilde in the previous paragraph – as well as the dangers of reducing art to a means to promote certain moral or political views, championed by religious institutions or ruling political elites, jeopardizing the freedom of artists to challenge established lifestyles and choices.

However, there are interesting differences between art forms in this respect. I do not want to deny that artworks, particularly movies, theatre plays and novels, can teach us something about morality and that under certain conditions this can be an aesthetic merit in them – a point developed and argued for by Berys Gaut.[101]

Economic value. Art is, among other things, also a commodity on a market where prices are influenced by supply and demand. But this market can also be manipulated by several activities. Staggering prices for the works of some artists at auctions are reported in the media – record after record is noted, while many other artists have a hard time making a living from their work.

Merda d'artista (Artist's Shit), 1961, by the Italian artist Piero Manzoni, is a spectacular example. The work consists of ninety tin cans, each stated to contain thirty grams of faeces. According to Wikipedia, on 16 October 2015, tin 54 was sold at Christie's for £182,500. In August 2016, at an art auction in Milan, one of the tins sold for a new record of €275,000, including the auction fee.

A time perspective is important here, since the economic value of a work of art can vary with time. During her lifetime, Frida Kahlo (1907–1954) only exhibited a few of her works. She could hardly imagine that one of her self-portraits would be sold for a record sum of over 30 million euros, approximately sixty years after her death. As is well known, van Gogh sold only one work during his lifetime – and that was to his brother Theo. Now his paintings are sold for millions of euros.

Therapeutic value. To create, perform or regard art can have therapeutic value. Art exhibited on the walls of hospitals can increase the well-being of patients and healthcare staff. Creative work can sometimes be a way to deal with traumatic experiences. When art is used to promote health, quality of life, communicative skills, or personal development, this value is a fairly obvious example of an instrumental value. Art is then used as a means to achieve or enhance other things, states of affairs or states of mind that are valued. There is a considerable literature on various forms of music therapy, for instance used for persons suffering from dementia.[102]

Historic value. Finally, works of art can have historic or affective value, depending on what or who the work is associated with. The work may document or be an object surviving from an important historic event, or it may have been created by a historically important person like Winston Churchill or belonged to Napoleon. It may also have been created by a close and loved relative, now no longer alive, and will therefore mean a lot to those who knew the artist.

It is not necessary to assume that AI programs have consciousness (experiences and intentions) for AI-generated pictures to have economic value. A unique or rare misprint (for instance, the wrong colour) of a stamp may increase the value of that stamp for collectors, provided there is a market for stamps. Analogously, it is not necessary to assume that AI programs have consciousness (experiences and intentions) for AI-generated pictures to have historic value in the sense outlined here. It seems thus difficult to exclude that AI-generated pictures can have or promote values of the three last kinds: economic, therapeutic and historic.

Combinations. The different kinds of values can be defined in several ways. A work can exhibit or promote one, more or all of these values. They can also be graded. What might be called 'the value component of art' can thus vary from work to work. Combinations of these values can be used to describe differences between different concepts of art as well as between different kinds of art. But such combinations can also be used to describe different art publics and their preferences – and to analyse differences between art forms.

Finally, I am not assuming that works of art are the only entities that can have, exhibit or promote the values mentioned here. However, some artworks may do this better than other human activities or states of affairs. The various kinds of values discussed here are to be used as analytic tools in the discussion of whether AI-generated pictures may be works of art – and if the answer is affirmative, what this would require.

Summing up some distinctions. The literature, particularly on the distinction between aesthetic and artistic value, is extensive.[103] The values mentioned in Sections 6.5 and 6.6 can be combined, as already mentioned; an artwork can have or promote several of these values. But it is also important to distinguish between them. As for the relations between aesthetic and artistic value, the analysis proposed here suggests the following theses:

(1) These values cannot be identified with each other.

The reason is that there are works with artistic value but without aesthetic value, for instance, some conceptual works of art; and there are objects with aesthetic value but without artistic value. Besides, there are objects with both aesthetic and artistic value, but 'their value as art is not exhausted by their aesthetic value'.[104]

(2) There is more than one distinction.

The reason is simply that there are different concepts of artistic and aesthetic value. Earlier, I distinguished between, for instance, artistic value defined in terms of communication of feelings (Tolstoy), in terms of originality (Young), and in terms of dialogue (Berger), and so forth. Thus, there is more than one distinction depending on what concept of artistic value is compared to what concept of aesthetic value.

(3) Artistic value is a convenient linguistic construction.

Insisting on the distinction between aesthetic and artistic value is compatible with the proposal by Hanson that 'artistic value' is a linguistic construction that makes it easier to talk about the extent to which something is good art: '"Artistic value", according to this view, is just a handy linguistic construction that allows one to talk about the degree to which something is good art in a less cumbersome way than would otherwise be available'.[105]

More generally, it could be argued that if a work of art can have both cognitive and aesthetic value, and if the interplay between these values is essential to the overall artistic value of that work of art, then aesthetic, artistic and cognitive value cannot be identified.

6.7 A Proposal

Is there a difference between artworks and mere real things? Arthur Danto has argued that: 'to see something as art is to be ready to interpret it in terms of what and how it means'.[106] 'Interpretation' is the key concept here for Danto. It helps to define the difference between artworks and mere real things.[107] This is in line with Danto's philosophy of art, which he summarizes as: 'finding the deep differences between art and craft, artworks and mere things, when members from either class look exactly similar'.[108]

An intentionalist conception of art can be developed in several ways, but it will roughly presuppose an intention to make or select something, and that whatever is made or selected is regarded or treated in certain ways. Such a conception of art has been developed by Jerrold Levinson in his intentionalist and historicist definition of art.

Levinson summarizes his main idea as follows: 'It is, in short, that an artwork is a thing that has been intended by someone for regard-as-a-work-of-art – i.e., regard in any *way preexisting artworks are or were correctly regarded.*'[109] Then he proposes and discusses various modifications and improvements of this definition. He concludes by adding the following somewhat vague clause to the summary of his main idea in the first sentence of this paragraph: *so that an experience of some value be thereby obtained.*[110]

In this context, this approach raises the question of who such intentions can be attributed to meaningfully: the user, the programmer, the trainer, the computer or the computer program? The latter ones, of course, are more controversial than the former ones.

Against this background, consider now the following proposal: having an intention to create an intentional object, an object about something that is regarded and treated in the same way as present and previously existing artworks, is necessary for the creation of art. Is this condition met by AI programs or algorithms? Does it have to be? Ajan Chatterjee – like Mazzone and Elgammal – argues that it is not necessary.[111] AI can produce art, in his view, even if it does not meet the proposed condition discussed in this paragraph.

Chatterjee acknowledges that AI might not understand ideas or experience emotions, but, nevertheless, it could be able to produce meaningful and evocative art. Nor does AI have to intend to make art. To succeed with this argument, it seems that Chatterjee has to neglect the distinction between aesthetic, artistic and other kinds of value artworks might have or promote. This criticism will also be relevant against Mazzone and Elgammal.

The challenge is to create or appreciate art without having intentions, experiencing emotions, or having any complex motivation of the sort that van Gogh, Picasso or Rothko had when they produced some of their best-known works. The solution, according to Chatterjee, is to develop a sophisticated list of labels based on features that people like in great art, thus going beyond the Facebook 'likes'. He continues: 'The point is that AI need not know what it is looking at or experience emotions. All it needs to be able to do is label a novel image with descriptions and impacts – a more complex version of labeling an image as a brown dog even if it has never seen that particular dog before'.[112]

But a possible objection against this solution has been expressed as follows by Boden: 'We don't ascribe artistic integrity to someone who produces art in indefinitely many styles on request (as some commercial graphic designers can do). . . . We say, rather, that they haven't found their own voice, or that their work has no unity.'[113]

This objection by Boden is, in the first place, relevant and effective against early AI programs like MidJourney, where the user can instruct the program to produce images of a certain motif, say a still life, in various styles (Renaissance, impressionist, minimalist, etc.) rather than against pictures produced by deep learning techniques and GANs. But if the difference between these types of picture-generating programs is one of degree rather than one of kind, this objection may also, to some extent, hit other types of picture-generating AI programs than the earlier ones.

Even so, there is a need to develop a more refined toolbox in view of the many people involved in the creation of what is labelled as art generated by AI programs. The idea is then simply to ask and specify who has contributed what, for instance using the previously mentioned conceptual framework pro-posed by Mackie.[114] Those who made such contributions could and should be considered as contributing authors of the work generated.

Is *Portrait of Edmond Belamy* art and even good art? Chatterjee answers that it is art.[115] He refers to the institutional theory of art for support. The fact that Christie's, one of the major auction houses, sold the *Portrait of Edmond Belamy* for nearly half a million US dollars is used as an argument by Chatterjee to support the claim that this AI-generated picture is accepted as an artwork by the art world: 'If our social institutions agree that an object is art, then it is. Being auctioned and sold by Christie's certainly qualifies as an institution claiming that AI art is in fact art.'[116]

But, as indicated elsewhere in this text, the decision and marketing by Christie's of this portrait turned out to be highly controversial and has sparked widespread critical comments.[117] Additionally, many strong arguments have been advanced against the institutional theory, summarized as 'art is what the art world considers to be art', including pointing out its circularity, the lack of clarity of the key notion 'the art world', and its neglect of the value dimension of art.

6.8 The Need for Hypothetical Answers

Margaret Boden argues that it is premature at present to take a categorical position on whether creativity and AI are a contradiction in terms,[118] as mentioned earlier. This is so because of the controversies surrounding the definitions and theories of some of the key concepts involved. Particularly important are controversies over definitions and theories about freedom (autonomy), intentionality, valuation, emotion, and consciousness.

The situation is in some ways similar when the focus of the discussion is AI and art. Here, controversies over definitions, criteria and theories of art are added to the list in the previous paragraph. Currently, what we can hope for at most are some hypothetical answers, where the answers are related to, and based on, a number of explicit assumptions. Further progress will require clarification – involving research and discussion – of the key concepts in these assumptions.

Furthermore, as discussed previously, due to the speed with which AI technologies are developing, what is not possible today may be possible tomorrow. It is difficult to hit a moving target. Thus, there is a need for hypothetical answers related to specific assumptions, in particular, about the technology and how it is to be described. The same is true for assumptions about art and creativity, as well as about the possibility and relevance of AI software having experiences or developing awareness of its intentions, emotions and values.

To see the need for hypothetical answers, it is instructive to compare the positions of Mazzone and Elgammal on the one hand and of Hertzmann on the other. While the first argue that the AI technology they describe – AICAN – is an almost autonomous artist, Hertzmann takes the view that at least at present, AI is just a tool for artists and not an artist itself. Hertzmann's main argument for his position makes explicit some of the assumptions he makes about art, schematically:

(1) Art is something created by social agents.
(2) A 'social agent' is anything that has a status akin to personhood: someone worthy of empathy and ethical consideration.

(3) Computers and AI systems are not social agents.

(4) Hence, computers cannot be credited with authorship of art in our current understanding.

However, terms like 'social agent' or 'social actor' can be interpreted in more than one way. In their study of attitudes towards artwork produced by humans versus those produced by AI, Joo-Wha Hong and Nathaniel Ming Curran use a theory according to which computers are social actors.[119] For Herzmann, a social agent is someone who has experiences that this social agent wants to share with others. Social interaction involves communication. But Hong and Curran clearly use 'social actor' in a different sense. They refer to studies indicating that people tend to 'perform social rules without thought when interacting with computers' and 'to treat computers as independent from their programmers'[120] The focus is here not on what the computer programs (the algorithms) do but on what those who use the computers do and think.

Does social interaction require consciousness? Let us assume that it does. However, as mentioned earlier, Elgammal and Mazzone argue – in an interesting comparison between Francis Bacon's distorted portraits and pictures of distorted faces created by AI – that the distortions are due to the fact that the software has failed to imitate the pictures fed into it, and that there is no intention of the program involved in the creation of these pictures.[121]

Thus, it seems that we can argue hypothetically and say:

(a) If intentions to share and communicate experiences are necessary, and the software has no such intentions, AI-generated pictures are not art, and the human user or possibly the software designer is the artist; the software is just a tool (Hertzmann).

  or

(b) If the AI program/software has no intentions, but intentions to share and communicate experiences are not necessary for creating art, AI-generated pictures may be art – if they exhibit other aesthetic or art-making properties, for instance like those described by Daniel Berlyne (Mazzone and Elgammal).

Here, Mazzone and Elgammal (2019) refer to the theory of Daniel Berlyne, but without making the important distinction between aesthetic and artistic value:

> Experimental psychologist Daniel Berlyne (1924–1976) studied the basics of the psychology of aesthetics for several decades and pointed out that *novelty, surprisingness, complexity, ambiguity* and *puzzlingness* are the most

significant properties in stimulus relevance to studying aesthetic phenomena . . .
Indeed, the resulting images with all the deformations in the faces are novel,
surprising and puzzling to us. In fact, they might remind us of Francis Bacon's
famous deformed portraits . . .

However, this comparison highlights a major difference, that of intent. It
was Bacon's intention to make the faces deformed in his portrait, but the
deformation we see in the AI art is not the intention of the artist nor of the
machine. Simply put, the machine fails to imitate the human face completely
and, as a result, generates surprising deformations.[122]

6.9 Tentative Conclusions

I will now return to some of the issues mentioned in the introduction of this
section and answer them tentatively. It will have important consequences for the
position taken on the main problem in this text ('Can computers create art?'),
which of the assumptions discussed in this text – or what particular combination
of them – are taken for granted, and how they are defined more precisely.

As for the process, having checked the assumptions on which various answers
to the issues raised in the introduction to this section may be based, my personal
view – like the view expressed by Hertzmann – is that the presently available AI
programs are or can be tools used by human artists. However, these programs are
not artists and should not be regarded as such; they do not qualify as artists.

As for the result, my conclusion is that no categorical answer can be given at the
present time, since any answer will have to rely on contested assumptions. I have
not been convinced that AI programs can be attributed the kind of autonomy,
awareness and sentience that would be required to regard the pictures generated as
works of art, at least according to some interpretations of artistic value.

But the pictures generated by AI tools can – as suggested earlier in the
discussion of the values that works of art can have – certainly have or promote
other kinds of value, including aesthetic and cognitive value, according to some
of the earlier discussed interpretations of these terms.

Can pictures generated by AI software be art? Those who answer in the
affirmative, like Mazzone and Elgammal,[123] may appear to be wrong according
to my view, mainly because the process of creation is so different and no
distinction is made by them between aesthetic and artistic value, between, on
the one hand, aesthetic objects and, on the other, art and its objects, which are
intentional as proposed by many philosophers of art.[124]

But a qualification – opening up for a less categorical answer – is immediately necessary. According to the Umbrella theory, artworks can have or
promote values of several kinds. These values can be defined in several ways
and also be combined in different proportions. Thus, a computer-generated

picture can be art in the sense that it exemplifies a combination of some of these values. The presence of a specific interpretation of 'artistic value', such as originality, is not in all cultures and at all times a necessary condition for something to be art. A definition of art could have the shape of a series of disjunctions, where it is enough to meet the requirements of some of the clauses of the disjunction.

Besides, art cannot be characterized as one kind of activity; it is many. It is a mistake to think that there is one single feature separating everything that is art (or is recognized as art) from what is not art. My view is that art promotes or exhibits many kinds of values, some may be aesthetic, but there are also others, especially cognitive and artistic. The latter of these values are particularly complex. Many versions of artistic value can be distinguished, each of which can be defined in several ways, as indicated earlier in the text.

The many varieties of art can also be seen if we take as a point of departure Sahlin's previously discussed theory of creativity with its (three) interrelated components: (a) breaking of rules, (b) inventing new concepts and (c) in order to solve or shed light on problems.[125] A pointillist painting can be said to be constructed according to the more or less precise implicit rules for paintings in this style. These rules can be derived from, and made explicit by analysing, the key paintings of the movement, such as *A Sunday Afternoon on the Island of Le Grande Jatte* by Georges Seurat. The rules broken can be of many kinds, as is indicated by a number of scandals in the history of art, also reflected in the originally pejorative or negatively intended labels used by unsympathetic critics for some of these rule-breaking new activities: 'baroque', 'mannerism', 'pointillism', 'fauvism', 'impressionism', and so on.

The development of art since the 1920s has shown that we need a new conceptual toolbox to talk about art in a way that is relevant to the concerns of artists and critics. The aesthetic dimension has been challenged. Not all contemporary art is beautiful, and not everything that is beautiful (such as sunsets or craft) is art. Do we need a new toolbox for pictures generated by AI programs? Some suggestions are indicated in Section 2. Moreover, during the history of art, artists at different times and in various cultures have tried to solve or shed light on different problems, some of which the artists may have been only dimly aware of themselves. Borders can be tested and lifestyle choices challenged by creating and exhibiting artworks.

Other problems include examination of the limits, if any, to artistic freedom and the role, if any, of ethical concerns in art. For instance, is everything acceptable in order to get the attention of the media, so important today for an artistic career? These are much-discussed issues at present, but in the past partly different issues were in focus. Some of these problems had to do with conflicts between the church, the state, political parties (the Nazis and 'entartete Kunst') and/or those with money and power. Giotto and van Eyck did not, by their works, shed light on or try to solve the same problems as Picasso, Salvador Dalí, or Andy Warhol, not to mention masters in other cultures like Mu Chi, a Chinese Chan Buddhist monk and painter who lived in the thirteenth century.

What about an open and cautious (such as: perhaps in the future, if . . . and if not . . .) answer to the question 'Can computers create art?' What would such a cautious answer require? The idea could simply be that in the future things may change due to the development of the technology and/or intensified collaboration between artists and software engineers.

The problem with such 'wait and see' arguments is that they are not only poor, but also difficult to refute, as Sahlin points out.[126] It is always possible to argue that things may be different in the future. Looking back at what the situation was before the Internet, television, and radio, it is tempting to agree, even if the complex factors that have an impact on development are unknown and hard to predict.

7 Concluding Remarks

7.1 Introduction

In this section, I will begin by describing some alleged dangers of certain ways of using AI tools to generate what is labelled as art, as well as some other dangers related to ways of talking about such uses. The need for transparency is then discussed briefly. I conclude with some comments on art and AI in the future.

7.2 Dangers

New technology in art has often been met with resistance, a point emphasized by several writers, including Hertzmann and Agüera y Arcas, as mentioned earlier. But with the benefit of hindsight, we can see that this negative attitude has often been unjustified. Photography is an instructive example.

Moreover, Hertzmann stresses that collaborations between artists and computer scientists can have a number of positive effects; new technology is not a threat or an enemy to art. 'One of my main goals in this essay has been to highlight the degree to which technology contributes to art, rather than being antagonistic.'[127] He adds, 'Today, we are seeing many intriguing and beguiling experiments with AI techniques; and, as artists' tools, they will surely transform the way we think about art in thrilling and unpredictable ways.'[128]

But he also warns against some dangers of certain ways of describing the use of these new technologies in making pictures:

A continual danger of new AI technology is that human users misunderstand the nature of the AI (O'Neil 2016). When we call a shallow AI an 'artist', we risk seriously misleading or lying to people. I believe that, if you convince people that an AI is an artist, then they will also falsely attribute emotions, feelings, and ethical weight to that AI. If this is true, I would argue calling such AIs 'artists' is unethical. It leads to all sorts of dangers, including overselling the competence and abilities of the AI, to misleading people about the nature of art.[129]

A different kind of danger was expressed by one of the participants in a YouTube movie from a webinar arranged by the Institute for Ethics in AI at Oxford: 'There is a danger that we will replace our own experience with a machine that has no experience.' But, of course, this presupposes a discussion of, and a position taken on, the basic assumption that machines can have experiences, an assumption discussed earlier and one that some philosophers and scientists apparently seem prepared to accept, while others do not.

Chatterjee also points to some dangers in the use of AI in the production and appreciation of art. For instance, he suggests that AI could be used by museums to predict what kind of art would draw most viewers and then 'narrow the range of art displayed', or be used by artists to 'shift their output to what AI predicts will sell'.[130] Moreover, Chatterjee writes that 'the ongoing development of aesthetically sensitive machines will challenge our views of beauty and creativity and perhaps our understanding of the nature of art'. He concludes his paper by writing: 'Ultimately, we do not know if sentient AI will be benevolent, malevolent, or apathetic when it comes to human concerns. We don't know if sentient AI will care about art.'[131]

7.3 The Need for Transparency

I agree with McCormack et al. that authors have a 'responsibility to accurately represent the process used to generate a work, including the labour of both machines and other people'.[132] The use of open source software does not change this. Incidentally, this recommendation about transparency and honesty is consistent with the recommendations in research generally, as stated in the *European Code of Conduct for Research Integrity.*[133]

Some of the economic and legal implications mentioned at the end of Section 1 can probably be dealt with by increasing the transparency about the way the pictures are produced, what software was used, who has contributed what, who is providing financial support and who may have any economic interests, as well as about the number of copies printed – and the numbering of each copy.

Several economic and legal issues in other areas, for instance involving aspects of cooperation between industry and academia, have, with some success, been dealt with through increased transparency. The market, including the art market, usually reacts negatively to uncertainty, which is why openness and transparency are essential. To deal with the legal issues, perhaps more distinctions and new conceptual tools might be helpful. There is room for creative collaboration between philosophers, legal scholars, artists and computer scientists concerning some of the implications mentioned at the end of Section 1.

What would increased transparency about the creation of new algorithms in advanced AI programs mean? Increased transparency about which values/preferences, and whose, are fed into the program? Is increased transparency at all possible? What would this require? Perhaps further development of the technology?

7.4 Art and AI in the Future

Hardly surprising, the controversies raised by the use of AI programs to make pictures also include speculations about the future, such as:

(a) Will AI-generated pictures in the future be recognized as art by the art world and/or the general public?

or

(b) Will increased collaboration between software engineers and artists in the future pave the way for attributing consciousness – including, in particular, awareness of intentions, emotions and values – to some advanced picture-generating AI programs?

Many contributions to the discussion of AI tools include such speculations. Examples include: 'As times progress, with women's suffrage, Indigenous citizenship, and increasing egalitarianism so too the granting of authorship has expanded. Perhaps when AIs are granted citizenship they too will receive legal recognition as authors ...'[134]

I have not spent much time on such speculations, since they are highly uncertain, difficult to refute and support convincingly – and tend to be coloured either by wishful thinking or by fears. The one thing that seems safe to say about art in the future is that the precise development of art during the coming decades and centuries cannot be predicted. However, three somewhat more general predictions can be made.

First, as several writers have suggested (Hertzmann, among others), there will be artists who will continue to work with traditional means and tools of art production (paints, brushes, clay, marble, pens, paper, etc.) along with artists who will explore the new possibilities offered by AI technologies.

Secondly, as mentioned by Hertzmann and others, it can also be assumed that the exploration of new tools and mediums will have a vitalizing effect on art. This has been the case previously when artists have explored the possibilities offered by earlier new technologies, like photography, now an art form in its own right.

Thirdly, an issue that is likely to get more attention in the future concerns the use of AI in art without critical reflection on the biases of the data and the patterns found in the data. This particular aspect of the use of AI in art has been discussed extensively by the media theorists Lev Manovich and Joanna Zylinska, as well as by Andreia Machado Oliveira.[135]

Referring to *Artificial Unintelligence* by Meredith Broussard, Machado Oliveira points out that with 'large-scale automation, made possible by the combination of artificial intelligence and digital networks, we can discern algorithms of oppression'.[136] If and when AI is used in the arts, we must not be naively uncritical: 'We have a responsibility to ask how computers interpret data, and when data is misinterpreted, to determine what is behind the erroneous programming.'[137]

Machado Oliveira illustrates the concerns some artists have about AI with regard to its social, political and ecological aspects with the following example.[138] The American artist Lauren Lee McCarthy has developed the performance *LAUREN* to demonstrate the biases behind the programming of AI by developers. In the performance, she becomes a version of Amazon's virtual assistant, Alexa, in order to show how AI guides decisions. This example is also discussed by Zylinska,[139] whose book is a critique of the socio-political underpinning of AI and the role of big tech companies sponsoring much of AI research and AI art. Thus, it has a different and broader scope than the present work.

The dangers discussed in the previous paragraph exemplify more general problems raised by AI. Obviously, the increasing use of AI raises questions as to what kind of society we want to live in and hand over to our children and grandchildren – and their children and grandchildren. In this text, I have focused on some more specific issues raised by the use of AI in art. But if the use of AI by artists will change current aesthetic and artistic standards and our ways of perceiving the world (for instance, by AI-created versions of movies), then we must be prepared to problematize the use of AI in art.

Notes

1. Rose (2022).
2. Schneider and Rea (2018).
3. Browne (2022: 130).
4. Browne (2022: 133).
5. Described by Sahlin (2006: 73).
6. Mazzone and Elgammal (2019: 1).
7. Mazzone and Elgammal (2019: 2).
8. Mazzone and Elgammal (2019: 3).
9. Mazzone and Elgammal (2019: 4).
10. McCormack et al. (2019: 13).
11. Herzmann (2018: 11; italics in original).
12. Herzmann (2018: 22).
13. Boden (2014: 233).
14. Boden (2010a: 181; italics in original).
15. Boden (2010a: 180).
16. Boden (2014: 230; italics in original).
17. Boden (2014: 236; italics in original).
18. Boden (2014: 236–237).
19. Gaut (2012: 119).
20. McCormack et al. (2019: 6).
21. Mazzone and Elgammal (2019: 5).
22. Mazzone and Elgammal (2019: 5).
23. McCormack et al. (2019).
24. Mackie (1974: 62; italics in original).
25. Browne (2022).
26. McCormack et al. (2019).
27. Boden (2010a: chapter 9).
28. Galanter (2020).
29. O'Hear (1995).
30. McCormack et al. (2019: 5).
31. Galanter (2020: 1).
32. Galanter (2020: 8).
33. Galanter (2020: 4).
34. Boden (2014).
35. McCormack et al. (2019: 12).
36. Glannon (2022: 1).
37. Glannon (2022: 1).
38. Glannon (2022: 2).
39. Glannon (2022: 58).
40. Galanter (2020: 4).
41. Dennett (2001, 2018).
42. Glannon (2022: 40).

43. Glannon (2022: section 2).
44. Gulik (2022) and Glannon (2022).
45. Gombrich (1960; particularly chapters II and V).
46. McCormack et al. (2019: 6).
47. Wind (1948: 3), Hermerén (1969: 163).
48. Glannon (2022: 58).
49. Agüera y Arcas (2017).
50. Agüera y Arcas (2017: 7).
51. Gunkel (2017: 263).
52. Tännsjö (2023).
53. Agüera y Arcas (2017: 4).
54. Agüera y Arcas (2017: 7).
55. Oliveira (2022: 210).
56. Agüera y Arcas (2017: 6).
57. Agüera y Arcas (2017: 6).
58. Sahlin (2006), Boden (2004, 2010a).
59. Sahlin (2006: 47).
60. Boden (2004: 3).
61. Boden (2010a: 72).
62. Boden (2014: 228).
63. Josephson (1991; first published 1955), Gombrich 1960).
64. Sahlin (2006).
65. Sahlin (2006: 47).
66. Sahlin (2006: 85).
67. Sahlin (2006: 78).
68. Sahlin (2006: 79–84).
69. See, for instance, Spalding (2012).
70. Fry (1963).
71. Boden (2014: 234–235).
72. Sahlin (2006: 56).
73. Sahlin (2006: 56).
74. Boden (2014).
75. Johansson (2004).
76. Sahlin (2006: 147–158).
77. Malina (2002: 464).
78. See for instance Carroll (2000), Levinson (2003).
79. Boden (2010b: 409.
80. Boden (2010b: 409.
81. Boden (2010b: 412).
82. Mazzone and Elgammal (2019: 4–5).
83. Mazzone and Elgammal (2019: 5).
84. Samo and Highhouse (2023: 8).
85. Boden (2010b: 411).
86. Gaut (2000, 2005).
87. Gaut (2007: 39).
88. Hermerén (2022).

89. Dickie (1971, 1974, 1984, 2001).
90. Berlyne (1971).
91. Tolstoy (1995; first published 1897).
92. Berger (2001).
93. Berger (2001: 16; italics in the original).
94. Berger (2001: 21).
95. Crowther (2007).
96. Crowther (2007: 56; italics in original).
97. Schellekens (2022).
98. Schellekens (2007: 73).
99. Klee (1920: 'Kunst gibt nicht das Sichtbare wieder, sondern Kunst macht sichtbar').
100. Gaut (2007).
101. Gaut (2007, chapters 7–10).
102. Van der Steen et al (2018).
103. For some earlier discussions, see Sibley (1959), Cohen (1973), Hermerén (1983: 53–76 and 1988); for later discussions see Goldman (1995), Vaida (1998), Gaut (2007: 26–41), Lopes (2011), Hanson (2013), Stecker (2012).
104. Stecker (2012: 355).
105. Hanson (2013: 500).
106. Danto (1992: 41).
107. This proposal is further developed by Danto in (1981: 1–33).
108. Danto (1992: 53).
109. Levinson (1990: 38–39; italics in original).
110. Levinson (1990: 56; italics in original).
111. Chatterjee (2022), Mazzone and Elgammal (2019).
112. Chatterjee (2022: 4).
113. Boden (2010a: 187).
114. Mackie (1974: 62).
115. Chatterjee (2022).
116. Chatterjee (2022: 7).
117. Among others McCormack et al. (2019) and Browne (2022).
118. Boden (2014).
119. Hong and Curran (2019).
120. Hong and Curran (2019, 58: 4).
121. Mazzone and Elgammal (2019: 2).
122. Mazzone and Elgammal (2019: 2).
123. Mazzone and Elgammal (2019).
124. Wollheim (1980).
125. Sahlin (2006).
126. Sahlin (2006: 89).
127. Herzmann (2018: 22).
128. Herzmann (2018: 22).
129. Herzmann (2018: 21).
130. Chatterjee (2022: 7).
131. Chatterjee (2022: 8).

132. McCormack et al. (2019: 13).
133. ALLEA (2023)
134. McCormack et al. (2019: 8).
135. Manovich (2019), Zylinska (2020) and Machado Oliveira (2022).
136. Oliveira (2022: 214).
137. Oliveira (2022: 214).
138. Oliveira (2022: 219).
139. Zylinska (2020: 137).

References

Agüera y Arcas, Blaise. Art in the Age of Machine Intelligence. *Arts* 6 (2017): 18. https://doi.org/10.3390/arts6040018.

ALLEA, All European Academies. *European Code of Conduct for Research Integrity*. Revised ed. Berlin: ALLEA, 2023.

Bell, Clive. *Art*. New York: Stokes, 1913.

Berger, John. *The Shape of a Pocket*. London: Penguin, 2001.

Berlyne, David. *Aesthetics and Psychology*. New York: Appleton-Century-Crofts of Meredith Corporation, 1971.

Boden, Margaret A. *The Creative Mind: Myths and Mechanisms*. 2nd ed. London: Routledge, 2004.

Boden, Margaret A. *Creativity and Art: Three Roads to Surprise*. Oxford: Oxford University Press, 2010a.

Boden, Margaret A. The Turing Test and Artistic Creativity. *Kybernetes* 39, 3 (2010b): 409–413. https://doi.org/10.1108/03684921011036132.

Boden, Margaret A. Creativity and Artificial Intelligence: A Contradiction in Terms? In Elliot Samuel Paul and Scott Barry Kaufman, eds., *The Philosophy of Creativity: New Essays*. Oxford: Oxford University Press, 2014: 224–244.

Broussard, Meredith. *Artificial Unintelligence: How Computers Misunderstand the World*. Cambridge, MA: MIT Press, 2018.

Browne, Kieran. Who (or What) Is an AI Artist? *Leonardo* 55, 2 (2002): 130–134. https://doi.org/10.1162/leon_a_02092.

Carroll, Noël, ed. *Theories of Art Today*. Madison: University of Wisconsin Press, 2000.

Chalmers, David J. *The Conscious Mind: In Search of a Fundamental Theory* (Philosophy of Mind Series). New York: Oxford University Press, 1996.

Chatterjee, Anjan. Art in an Age of Artificial Intelligence. *Frontiers in Psychology* 13 (2022): 1–9. https://doi.org/10.3389/fpsyg.2022.1024449.

Cohen, Ted. Aesthetics/Non-aesthetics and the Concept of Taste: A Critique of Sibley's Position . *Theoria* 39 (1973): 113–152.

Crowther, Paul. *Defining Art, Creating the Canon: Artistic Value in an Era of Doubt*. Oxford: Oxford University Press, 2007.

Danto, Arthur. *The Transfiguration of the Commonplace*. Cambridge, MA: Harvard University Press, 1981.

Danto, Arthur. *Beyond the Brillo Box*. Berkeley: University of California Press, 1992.

Dennett, Daniel. The Zombic Hunch: Extinction of an Intuition? In A. O'Hear, ed., *Philosophy at the New Millennium*. Cambridge: Cambridge University Press, 2001: 27–43.

Dennett, Daniel. Facing Up to the Hard Question of Consciousness. *Philosophical Transactions B* 373 (2018): 1–7. http://dx.doi.org/10.1098/rsb.2017.0342. Accessed 22 August 2023.

Dickie, George. *Aesthetics: An Introduction*. Indianapolis: Pegasus, Bobbs-Merrill, 1971.

Dickie, George. *Art and the Aesthetic*. Ithaca: Cornell University Press, 1974.

Dickie, George. *The Art Circle*. New York: Haven, 1984.

Dickie, George. *Art and Value*. Malden, MA: Blackwell, 2001.

Fry, Roger. *Cézanne: A Study of His Development*. New York: The Noonday Press, 1963.

Galanter, Philip. Towards Ethical Relationships with Machines That Make Art. In Andrés Burbano and Ruth West, coord. , 'AI, Arts & Design: Questioning Learning Machines'. *Artnodes* 26 (2020): 1–9. UOC. [Accessed 28 July 2023]. http://doi.org/10.7238/a.v0i26.3371.

Gaut, Berys. 'Art' as a Cluster Concept. In N. Carroll, ed., *Theories of Art Today*. Madison: University of Wisconsin Press, 2000: 15–44.

Gaut, Berys. The Cluster Account of Art Defended. *British Journal of Aesthetics* 43 (2005): 273–288. Doi:10.1093/aesthj/ayi032.

Gaut, Berys. *Art, Emotion and Ethics*. Oxford: Clarendon Press, 2007.

Gaut, Berys. Review of Margaret A. Boden, Creativity and Art. *British Journal of Aesthetics* 52 (2012): 116–119. https://doi.org/10.1093/aesthj/ayr041.

Glannon, Walter. *Ethics of Consciousness*. Cambridge: Cambridge University Press, 2022.

Goldman, Alan. *Aesthetic Value*. Boulder, CO: Westview Press, 1995.

Gombrich, Ernst H. *Art and Illusion*. London: Phaidon, 1960.

Goodfellow, Ian et al. Generative Adversarial Nets. Paper presented at the Advances in Neural Information Processing Systems, Montreal, QC, Canada, 8–13 December 2014.

Gunkel, David J. Special Section: Rethinking Art and Aesthetics in the Age of Creative Machines. Editor's Introduction. *Philosophy & Technology* 30 (2017): 263–265. https://doi.org/10.1007/s13347-017-0281-3.

Hanson, Louise. The Reality of (Non-aesthetic) Artistic Value. *The Philosophical Quarterly* 63, 252 (2013): 492–508. https://.jstor.org/stable/24672487.

Hermerén, Göran. *Representation and Meaning in the Visual Arts*. Lund: Scandinavian University Books, 1969.

Hermerén, Göran. *Aspects of Aesthetics*. (Acta Regiae Societatis Humaniorum Litterarum Lundensis LXXVII). Lund: LiberFörlag/Gleerup, 1983.

Hermerén, Göran. *The Nature of Aesthetic Qualities*. Lund: Lund University Press, 1988.

Hermerén, Göran. Konst, konstvärlden och konstvärden. *Lund: Vetenskapssocietetens Årsbok* (2022): 63–83.

Herzmann, Aaron. Can Computers Create Art? *Arts* 7, 18 (2018): 1–25. https://doi.org/10.3390/arts7020018.

Honderich, Ted. *How Free Are You?* Oxford: Oxford University Press, 1993.

Hong, Joo-Wha and Curran, Nathaniel Ming. Artificial Intelligence, Artists and Art: Attitudes Toward Artwork Produced by Humans vs. Artificial Intelligence. *ACM Transactions on Multimedia Computing, Communications, and Applications* 15 (2019): 1–16. https://doi.org/10.1145/3326337.

Johansson, Mats. *Empatisk förståelse: Från inlevelse till osjälviskhet.* Lund: Filosofiska institutionen, 2004.

Josephson, Ragnar. *Konstverkets födelse.* Lund: Studentlitteratur, 1991 (first published 1955).

Klee, Paul. *Schöpferische Konfession*. Berlin: Erich Reiss Verlag, 1920.

Levinson, Jerrold. *Music, Art, and Metaphysics*. Ithaca: Cornell University Press, 1990.

Levinson, Jerrold, ed. *The Oxford Handbook of Aesthetics*. Oxford: Oxford University Press, 2003.

Lopes, Dominic McIver. The Myth of (Non-aesthetic) Artistic Value. *The Philosophical Quarterly* 61, 244 (2011): 518–536. https://www.jstor.org/stable/23012980.

Machado Oliveira, Andreia. Future Imaginings in Art and Artificial Intelligence. *Journal of Aesthetics and Phenomenology* 9, 2 (2022): 209–225. https://doi.org/10.1980/20539320.2022.2150467.

Mackie, John L. *The Cement of the Universe*. Oxford: Clarendon Press, 1974.

Malina, Roger. The Stone Age of the Digital Arts. *Leonardo* 35 (2002): 463–465. https://doi.org/10.1145/3347092.

Manovich, Lev. *AI Aesthetics*. Moscow: Strelka Press, 2019.

Mazzone, Marian and Elgammal, Ahmed. Art, Creativity, and the Potential of Artificial Intelligence. *Arts* 8 (2019): 1–9. https://doi.org/10.3390/arts8010026.

McCormack, Jon, Gifford, Toby and Hutchings, Patrick. Autonomy, Authenticity, Authorship and Intention in Computer Generated Art. *arXiv*:1903.02166v1 [cs. AI] 6 March 2019. https://doi.org/10.1007/978-3-030-16667-0_3.

O'Hear, Anthony. Art and Technology: An Old Tension. In R. Fellows, ed., *Philosophy and Technology*. Cambridge: Cambridge University Press, 1995: 143–158.

Rose, Kevin. An A.I.-Generated Picture Won an Art Prize: Artists Aren't Happy. *The New York Times* 2 September 2022.

Sahlin, Nils-Eric. *Kreativitetens filosofi*. Nora: Nya Doxa, 2006.

Samo, Andrew and Highhouse, Scott. Artificial Intelligence and Art: Identifying the Aesthetic Judgment Factors that Distinguish Human- and Machine-Generated Artwork. *Psychology of Aesthetics, Creativity, and the Arts* (2023): 1–15. https://dx.doi.org/10.1037/aca0000570.

Schellekens, Elisabeth. The Aesthetic Value of Ideas. In Peter Goldie and Elisabeth Schellekens, eds., *Philosophy and Conceptual Art*. Oxford: Oxford University Press, 2007: 71–91.

Schellekens, Elisabeth. Conceptual Art. *Stanford Encyclopedia of Philosophy*, 2022. https://plato.stanford.edu/entries/conceptual-art/.

Schneider, Tim and Rea, Naomi. Has Artificial Intelligence Given Us the Next Great Art Movement? Experts Say Slow Down, the 'Field Is in Its Infancy'. *Artnet* 25 September 2018.

Sibley, Frank. Aesthetic Concepts. *Philosophical Review* 68 (1959): 421–450; reprinted, with revisions, in Joseph Margolis, ed., *Philosophy Looks at the Arts*. Philadelphia: Temple University Press, 1987; and in his *Approach to Aesthetics*, ed. John Benson, Betty Redfern and Jeremy Roxbee Cox. Oxford: Clarendon Press, 2001.

Spalding, Julian. *Sell Your Damien Hirsts while You Can*. Scotts Valley: CreateSpace Independent Publishing Platform, 2012.

Stecker, Robert. Artistic Value Defended. *Journal of Aesthetics and Art Criticism* 70, 4 (2012): 355–362.

Tännsjö, Torbjörn. Människan är inte unik. *Dagens Nyheter* 2 June 2023.

Tolstoy, Leo. *What Is Art?* London: Penguin, 1995 (first published 1897).

Vaida, Juliana Corina. The Quest for Objectivity: Secondary Qualities and Aesthetic Qualities. *Journal of Aesthetics and Art Criticism* 56 (1998): 283–297. https://www.jstor.org/stable/43496530.

Van der Steen, Jenny T, Smaling, Hanneke J A, van der Wouden, Johannes C et al. Music-Based Therapeutic Interventions for People with Dementia. *Cochrane Database of Systematic Reviews* 7 (2018): 1–99. Art No: CD003477.

Van Gulick, Robert. Consciousness. *The Stanford Encyclopedia of Philosophy* (Winter 2022 Edition), Edward N. Zalta & Uri Nodelman (eds.). https://plato.stanford.edu/archives/win2022/entries/consciousness/.

Wind, Edgar. *Bellini's Feast of the Gods*. Cambridge, MA: Harvard College Library, 1948.

Wollheim, Richard. *Art and Its Objects*. 2nd edition. New York: Cambridge University Press, 1980.

Young, Edward. *Conjectures on Original Composition*. Reprinted: Franklin Classics 2018 (first published in 1759).

Zylinska, Joanna. *AI Art: Machine Visions and Warped Dreams*. London: Open Humanities Press, 2020.

Acknowledgements

I want to thank Nils-Eric Sahlin and Steve Latham for helpful comments on earlier versions of this text, and Alan Crozier for checking an earlier version of my English manuscript.

Cambridge Elements ≡

Bioethics and Neuroethics

Thomasine Kushner
California Pacific Medical Center, San Francisco

Thomasine Kushner, PhD, is the founding Editor of the *Cambridge Quarterly of Healthcare Ethics* and coordinates the International Bioethics Retreat, where bioethicists share their current research projects, the Cambridge Consortium for Bioethics Education, a growing network of global bioethics educators, and the Cambridge-ICM Neuroethics Network, which provides a setting for leading brain scientists and ethicists to learn from each other.

About the Series

Bioethics and neuroethics play pivotal roles in today's debates in philosophy, science, law, and health policy. With the rapid growth of scientific and technological advances, their importance will only increase. This series provides focused and comprehensive coverage in both disciplines consisting of foundational topics, current subjects under discussion and views toward future developments.

Cambridge Elements$^{\equiv}$

Bioethics and Neuroethics

Elements in the Series

Responsibility for Health
Sven Ove Hansson

Roles of Justice in Bioethics
Matti Häyry

Bioethics, Public Reason, and Religion: The Liberalism Problem
Leonard M. Fleck

Controlling Love: The Ethics and Desirability of Using 'Love Drugs'
Peter Herissone-Kelly

Pathographies of Mental Illness
Nathan Carlin

Immune Ethics
Walter Glannon

What Placebos Teach Us about Health and Care: A Philosopher Pops a Pill
Dien Ho

The Methods of Neuroethics
Luca Malatesti and John McMillan

Antinatalism, Extinction, and the End of Procreative Self-Corruption
Matti Häyry and Amanda Sukenick

Philosophical, Medical, and Legal Controversies About Brain Death
L. Syd M Johnson

Conscientious Objection in Medicine
Mark Wicclair

Art and Artificial Intelligence
Göran Hermerén

A full series listing is available at: www.cambridge.org/EBAN

For EU product safety concerns, contact us at Calle de José Abascal, 56–1°, 28003 Madrid, Spain or eugpsr@cambridge.org.